STUDY GUIDE

Managerial Economics

Analysis • Problems • Cases

Eighth Edition

Lila J. Truett
Professor of Economics
The University of Texas at San Antonio

Dale B. Truett
Professor of Economics
The University of Texas at San Antonio

JOHN WILEY & SONS, INC.

To order books or for customer service call 1-800-CALL-WILEY (225-5945).

ISBN 0-471-46247-0

Printed in the United States of America.

10 9 8 7 6 5

Printed and bound Victor Graphics, Inc.

PREFACE

In order to do a good job of learning managerial economics, it is necessary to practice working problems related to the decision processes that are important for the success of a business firm. Most instructors who teach managerial economics using the Truett and Truett textbook spend a great deal of time demonstrating how to go about solving the kinds of economic problems managers face. However, no one is very likely to become proficient at solving these problems just by watching the instructor do the work. In a way, managerial economics is a lot like tennis or playing a musical instrument. Understanding how someone else does it and doing it yourself are two different things!

There was no workbook to accompany the first two editions of our textbook, but we advised both instructors and students to take advantage of the problem-solving approaches provided in each chapter and in the end-of-chapter materials. Instructors and students always responded positively, but we also had many requests for additional exercises that students could work outside of class. Because of this, we decided to prepare a comprehensive and innovative **Study Guide**. The Study Guide has been well received, and we hope that users of this new and reorganized release of it will continue to find it very helpful. It is uniquely suited to accompany our text, since most of the problems contained herein were modelled after exams, quizzes, and exercises employed in our own classes.

DESIGN AND FEATURES OF THE GUIDE

Each of the following chapters begins with a **Programmed Review**. After reading the corresponding chapter in the textbook, you should try to cover up the side of the page that contains the answers to the review and fill in the missing words. You should find that the reviews help you consolidate your thoughts about what each chapter covers and the key analytical devices it introduces.

In most chapters, the programmed reviews are followed by **Practice Problems**. The problems in these sets are carefully correlated to those that appear in the end-of-chapter materials found in the text. Each section heading in the set of practice problems contains a reference to the end-of-chapter problem or problems that are similar to what follows. For example, if you turn to page 17 in this Guide, you will see a topic heading followed in parentheses by "ref. EOCP 1, 3." This is an indication that end-of-chapter problems 1 and 3 from Chapter 2 of the text are similar to those that you will find under that heading in the Guide. Any time you see the "EOCP" reference, it will lead you to related problems at the end of the same chapter in the textbook.

You should note that some practice problems, like some of the text's end-of-chapter problems (those numbered C1, C2, etc.), require calculus. Whenever this is true, you will find a clear warning to that effect. (See p. 23 of the Guide, for example.) If your instructor is not using the calculus approach, you may wish to skip these problems.

The practice problems contain another special feature. Many of them are accompanied by a brief paragraph entitled **"Getting Started."** This paragraph helps you determine what steps you will need to take to solve the problem. If you have trouble putting the pieces of a problem together, this should be a feature that will help you out.

Each chapter of the Guide contains a few **Multiple Choice Questions** to familiarize you with the way this device could be employed on tests or quizzes. These are usually found following the practice problems. (In chapters that do not have practice problems, the multiple choice questions follow the programmed review.)

The final element of each chapter that has practice problems is a set of **Hand-In Problems**. These are intended for instructor use, and many of them require that the instructor supply one or more key numbers necessary to solve the problem. The pages of the Guide have been perforated to make it easy for you to tear out the hand-in problems, should your instructor choose to use this feature. Do not attempt to use the hand-in problems as additional exercises, since most require that the missing numbers be carefully specified in order to yield a meaningful solution.

SOLUTIONS FOR PRACTICE PROBLEMS AND ANSWERS TO MULTIPLE CHOICE QUESTIONS

This section of the Guide begins on p. 237. It contains not only the solution values for all the problems but also the step-by-step solutions themselves. While these may prove extremely useful to you in learning how to solve managerial economics problems, we do have one caution. Make your best effort to solve each problem yourself before consulting the step-by-step solutions. Really wrestle with getting the problem formulated, since this is about half the battle. It is useless to try to "learn" the solutions, since they are just the result of understanding the problem and setting it up correctly. When you are really getting the hang of it, you will probably find that you can make up a problem of your own and solve it.

ACKNOWLEDGMENTS

This Guide was written in its entirety by Dale and Lila Truett, the co-authors of the textbook, Managerial Economics, published by John Wiley and Sons, Inc. For his advice and suggestions on earlier editions of this work, we thank our friend and colleague, Dr. Dennis Hanseman. In addition, many thanks are owed our son, Patrick Truett, for his work on certain parts of the word processing that went into the final product.

TABLE OF CONTENTS

CHAPTER 1: Introduction, Basic Principles, and Methodology

Programmed Review

This introductory chapter discusses economics as an analytical tool for managers. One of its main objectives is to present a set of economic principles that can be applied to issues associated with solving managerial problems, beginning with the principle that the role of managers is to make _____. Another important principle is that these are always among _____, although one type of alternative is between choosing a given action as opposed to doing _____. A third principle related to decisions is that decisions always have _____ as well as _____. To make a rational decision, one must consider both of these, using the marginal or _____ approach to determine which alternative provides the best result.

decisions

alternatives

nothing
costs
benefits

incremental

That the anticipated objective of managers is to maximize the _____ of the firm is a fourth managerial principle. Sometimes managers make decisions that violate this maxim, since the relation between managers and shareholders presents a _____-agent problem. This occurs because what is good for shareholders may not be in the personal interests of managers. Not surprisingly, the value of the firm is based on its expected _____, a stream of returns that occurs in the future. This is a fifth important economic principle for managers.

value

principal

profits

Of course, a firm's total profit for a given time period depends on the difference between its revenue and its cost. The firm's revenue depends on the _____ for its product, a sixth

demand

important economic principle for managers. Its
cost, for any chosen output level, depends on
how it produces its output and what it pays (or
sacrifices) to get its inputs. For the level of
output it chooses, it must _____ its cost   minimize
in order for profit to be maximized. (Principle
No. 7).

Three additional principles were introduced
in the chapter. They are that the firm must
develop a strategy consistent with its market (No.
8), that the firm's growth depends on rational
investment decisions (No. 9), and that successful
firms deal rationally and ethically with laws
and regulations (No. 10).

This chapter also presented the problem-
solving approach used in the text and in the field
of managerial economics generally. It involves
four steps. These are (1) identification of the
problem, (2) a statement of the alternative
_____ to the problem, (3) determination of   solutions
what _____ are relevant to obtain the solution,   data
and (4) choosing the best possible solution.
The number of alternatives available to management
with respect to any given problem is a function
of time. Generally, the more time available to
deal with a specific problem, the more varied
the solutions may be.

The chapter ended with a brief discussion of
the basics of demand and supply. A demand
schedule or demand _____ shows the amounts of   curve
a good (service) that a buyer or group of buyers
will purchase over some time period at various
possible prices of the item. The amount that
will be purchased at a given price is called the

quantity _____ of the good. A change in a   demanded
variable other than the own price of the good
(change in a *determinant of demand*) will cause
the demand curve to _____.   This movement   shift
is called a change in _____. If the good's   demand
own price changes while all other variables remain
constant, a movement *along* the demand curve
occurs. This is called a change in _____   quantity
_____. A demand curve is normally expected   demanded
to slope downward to the right due to the _____   law
of demand, which says that people will buy more
of a good if its price is lowered.

A supply curve shows the amounts of a good
(service) that sellers are willing and able to
offer for sale at various possible prices. The
supply curve is frequently expected to slope
_____ to the right, indicating that sellers   upward
will increase quantity _____ if price   supplied
increases. In a market characterized by perfect
_____ equilibrium occurs at a price that   competition
equates quantity supplied with quantity _____.   demanded
If price is below equilibrium,   there will be
a _____ in the market for the good, and   shortage
price will rise. However, a price that is higher
than the equilibrium one will lead to a _____,   surplus
and price will fall. Many markets are not
perfectly competitive. Nevertheless, the way
price is established in a perfectly competitive
market provides insights that can be used to
analyze other types of markets.

QUESTIONS and PROBLEMS

1. In the recent past, General Motors Corporation (GM) has pur-
    chased interests in producers such as Daewoo in Korea and Fiat
    in Italy. In January, 2003, with the death of Mr. Giovanni
    Agnelli, long-time head of Fiat, General Motors was consider-
    ing a complete takeover of the Italian company's car-producing
    divisions. Those divisions, at the time, were losing money
    and plagued with labor problems. How is the proposed take-
    over related to the overall issue of managerial decision mak-
    ing in today's world?

Problems Relating to Value of the Firm

2. In 2003, Alicia Smyth was trying to choose between an invest-
    ment in two homebuilding firms, Coughlin and Baker (CB), and
    Stellar Homes (SH).   Her stockbroker was recommending CB,
    but she found an independent research report that showed the
    following data on projected profits.

Year	Profit of CB	Profit of SH
2004	$1,200,000	$1,800,000
2005	1,300,000	1,900,000
2006	2,000,000	1,900,000
2007	2,100,000	1,900,000
2008	2,200,000	2,100,000

    Ms. Smyth believed that she could expect a return of 6 percent
    per year on alternative investments of equal risk.

    a. Analyze the two profit streams using the present value
        formula introduced in Chapter 1 of the text, and determine
        whether Ms. Smyth should have followed her broker's
        advice.

b. Explain your result and how it relates to the fact that CB's profits are larger than SH's in three of the five years.

Getting Started:
This problem can be answered with hand calculations. However, it is also a good problem for you to do with a spreadsheet program such as Excel. The reason is that you will have to make three calculations for each year, starting with the value of $(1.06)^t$. Once you have a column for that value, you can apply it to each year's profit for each firm.

3. Let's revisit the two home building firms in the preceding problem. Recall that while SH had a healthy stream of profits, it was evident that CB was growing quickly. Now let's assume that the two firms are active in the same markets and that SH wishes to counter CB's expansion in those markets by lowering the selling prices of SH-built homes. Discuss the circumstances under which this might be an economically rational strategy, relating your answer to (a) the "law of demand," (b) the objective of profit maximization, and (c) the difference between near-term returns (payments) and future returns.

Problems On Basic Demand and Supply Analysis
    (ref. EOCP 1 through 5)

4. Below are hypothetical demand and supply curves for eyeglas-
    ses.

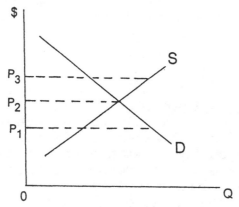

    Answer the following questions:

    a. Of the three prices given, which one is the equilibrium
        price? Why?

    b. What is the relation between quantity demanded and quan-
        tity supplied when the price is P_1?

    c. What is the relationship between quantity demanded and
        quantity supplied when the price is P_3?

    d. What will happen in the diagram if the prices that
        opthamologists charge for laser corrective eye surgery
        decrease by a substantial amount?

e. What will happen in the diagram if the cost of materials used in the manufacture of eyeglass lenses increases?

Getting Started:
        Keep in mind that the equilibrium price will equate quantity demanded with quantity supplied. At any other price, one of these quantities will exceed the other. Also, a change in a variable other than the price of eyeglasses will shift one of the curves.

5.   The table below gives demand and supply data for pears in a particular metropolitan market area. (Quantities in lbs. per week.)

Price Per Lb. In Cents	Quantity Demanded	Quantity Supplied	$(Q_s - Q_d)$
90	200	1,700	_____
80	400	1,400	_____
70	600	1,100	_____
60	800	800	_____
50	1,000	500	_____
40	1,200	200	_____

a. What is the equilibrium price of pears in this market, and how many pounds will be bought?

b. Complete the column $(Q_s - Q_d)$.

c. What kind of situation prevails when there is a positive number in the right-hand column? When the number is negative?

d. Explain how the market would adjust if price were at 70 cents per lb.

6. The market demand and supply curves for basic 17" CRT computer monitors have the following equations. (P is the price per unit, and Q is the quantity sold per month.)

Demand: $Q = 4,000,000 - 10,000P$

Supply: $Q = -1,000,000 + 40,000P$

a. Calculate the quantities demanded and supplied at a price of $180. Is this an equilibrium price? Explain.

b. Calculate the quantities demanded and supplied at a price of $100. Is this an equilibrium price? Explain.

Getting Started:
Before you do parts a and b, you might want to just set quantity demanded equal to quantity supplied using the given equations. Solving that will answer one of the two questions posed.

MULTIPLE CHOICE
   Circle the letter that corresponds to the best answer.

1. The reason much of managerial economics derives from microeconomics rather than macroeconomics is that:
    (a) it deals with general business conditions in the economy;
    (b) it considers broad industry trends rather than the operations of individual firms;
    (c) the process of decision making by the managers of an individual firm is its primary focus;
    (d) government policy is not a relevant variable to the individual firm.

2. The use of performance-based stock option plans and related types of rewards for managers is evidence of:
    (a) fraud and corruption in business firms;
    (b) the breech between theory and reality in economics;
    (c) the reasonableness of the assumtion of profit maximization;
    (d) shareholders' desires to make managers' goals consistent with their own.

3. Managerial economics makes broad use of marginal or incremental analysis because:

    (a) it indicates whether a change undertaken by the firm yields net gains;
    (b) there is really no other way to approach a business problem;
    (c) it is the only type of analysis ever used by economists;
    (d) it deals only with short-run and not long-run problems.

4. Only one of the following will increase the quantity demanded of new cars. Which one is it?

    (a) A fall in interest rates on new car loans.
    (b) An increase in consumers' incomes.
    (c) A decrease in income taxes.
    (d) A decrease in the average price of new cars.

5. Suppose the demand curve for electric power remains unchanged when an increase in the price of coal takes place. If the price of electric power does not change, we can expect that:
    (a) consumers will increase their use of electricity.
    (b) consumers will decrease their use of electricity.
    (c) there will be a shortage of electricity.
    (d) producers will increase the quantity supplied of electricity.

Chapter 1

HAND-IN PROBLEMS

Name_____

Course No. and Section_____

Problem 1.

Assume that the demand and supply curves in a given competitive market are described by the following equations.

Demand: $Q = $ _____ $- 30P$
                    (instructor-supplied number)

Supply: $Q = 500 + 10P$

a.   Explain why a price of $240 is not an equilibrium price in this market.

b.   Explain why a price of $160 is not an equilibrium price in this market.

c.   Determine the equilibrium price and quantities demanded and supplied in this market.

Chapter 1

HAND-IN PROBLEMS

Name_____

Course No. and Section_____

Problem 2.

A researcher has estimated that the local collector market for a particular, rare, "bobblehead" figure of a well-known retired sports star has the following demand and supply curves. (Quantities are number bought or sold per month.)

Supply: Q = _____ + 5P
           (instructor-supplied number)

Demand: Q = 420 - 5P

a.   Complete the table below.

Quantity Demanded	Price	Quantity Supplied	Surplus (+) or Shortage (-)
20	80	320	_____
_____	70	_____	_____
_____	60	_____	_____
_____	50	_____	_____
_____	40	_____	_____
_____	30	_____	_____
_____	20	_____	_____

b.   Determine the combination of price and quantity that corresponds to market equilibrium. Explain *why* this constitutes an equilibrium.

c.   The above-mentioned retired star is elected to the Hall of Fame. What do you expect to happen to the data in the table?

CHAPTER 2: Revenue of the Firm

Programmed Review

This chapter deals with the relation between the business firm's revenue from sales and consumer demand for the firm's product. The mathematical statement that relates the quantity of a good (service) that consumers are willing and able to purchase per time period to the independent variables that determine it is called the

_____ _____.   Relevant demand variables   <u>demand</u> <u>function</u>
include income, the prices of related goods, advertising, credit terms, and of course, the own
_____ of the good in question.   <u>price</u>

The demand curve for a given good or service shows how quantity demanded is related to the product's own price, assuming that all other demand function variables remain _____.   If   <u>constant</u>
the own price of the good remains constant but some other variable, such as income, changes, the demand curve will shift.   A shift of a
demand curve is called a _____ __ _____,   <u>change</u> <u>in</u> <u>demand</u>
but a movement along a given demand curve is a
change in _____ _____.   <u>quantity</u> <u>demanded</u>

Another name for price is _____ revenue.   <u>average</u>
When price is multiplied by quantity demanded, the result is called _____ _____. The   <u>total</u> <u>revenue</u>
rate of change of total revenue as quantity sold
changes is called _____ revenue. For a   <u>marginal</u>
straight-line demand curve, total revenue will
be maximized when marginal revenue is _____.   <u>zero</u>
For tabular data, it is appropriate to calculate <u>arc</u> marginal revenue as change in total revenue
divided by change in _____ _____.   <u>quantity</u> <u>demanded</u>

A straight-line demand curve can be described by the equation $P = a - bQ$, where a is the dollar

axis intercept of the curve, and *-b* is its slope.
Marginal revenue for such a curve is another
straight line with the same dollar axis
_____ and twice the negative _____.   intercept slope

The behavior of total revenue as price is decreased or increased can be predicted using the
coefficient of price _____ of demand. If   elasticity
total revenue increases as price is cut, the own
price elasticity will have an absolute value that
is _____ than 1.0. However, price cuts will   greater
reduce total revenue if the price elasticity is
_____ than 1.0 in absolute value. Elasticity   less
coefficients can be calculated for other demand
function variables (income, prices of related
goods, etc.) to see how _____ quantity   responsive
sold is to each variable. In the case of related
goods, the cross elasticity coefficient will be
positive if two goods are _____ but will   substitutes
have a negative sign if they are _____.   complements
It is important to distinguish between point and
arc elasticity. If the equation of the demand
curve for a specific good is known, point
elasticity can easily be calculated. For a single observed change in price and quantity taken,
the arc elasticity formula gives the _____   average
elasticity over the arc.

Although it is important to know whether a
given change in price will increase or decrease
total revenue, to assess the impact of price
changes on profit, a firm must also consider how
production _____ change as output rises or   costs
falls. Thus, demand and revenue are only one
building block in the economic analysis of the
firm.

PRACTICE PROBLEMS

Basic Problems on Demand and Revenue (ref. EOCP 1, 3).

1. The table below gives price and corresponding quantity demanded data for a firm:

Price (P)	Quantity Demanded (Q)	Total Revenue (TR)	Arc Marginal Revenue (MR)
16	0		
14	10		
12	20		
10	30		
8	40		
6	50		
4	60		
2	70		
0	80		

a. Complete the table by finding total revenue and arc marginal revenue.

b. Graph the curves of AR, MR and TR in the blank quadrants on the following page. Be sure to label units appropriately on each axis and to plot MR at the mid-point of each change in quantity.

> Getting Started:
> Fill in the TR column from the definition of total revenue. Then do the same for arc MR, which is change in TR divided by change in Q.

Graphs for Problem 1, section (b)

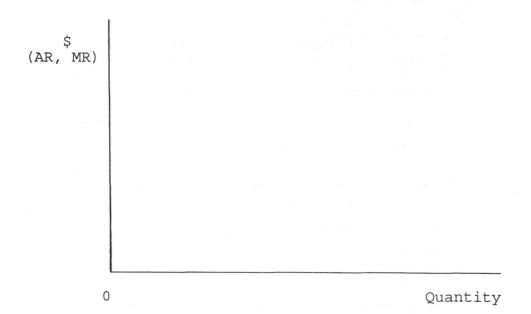

2. Starting from the definition of elasticity, derive the formula for the arc elasticity of demand for a good with respect to changes in its own price.

Getting Started:
        In English, say what elasticity tells about the relation of quantity demanded to changes in price. Now translate to symbols.

3. Complete the table below by finding total revenue and price.

Arc MR	Total Revenue (TR)	Quantity Demanded (Q)	Price (P)
		0	115
110			
		5	
100			
		10	
90			
		15	
80			
		20	
70			
		25	
60			
		30	

(continued next page)

a. Is there any range of data in this table where demand is elastic? Inelastic? Explain.

b. What is the arc elasticity of demand for the product in the table over the quantity range $Q = 20$ to $Q = 25$?

Getting Started:
Remember that arc MR tells the change in TR per unit that occurs when Q changes by a certain number of units (in this case, five). You can add up the changes in TR to get the total for any change in Q.
   For part (a), look at arc MR and relate to the elasticity.
   Use the arc elasticity formula for part (b).

4. The demand curve for good X is estimated to be the following.

$$Q_X = 800 - 25P_X$$

a. Rewrite the equation with price or average revenue (AR) as a function of quantity.

b. Write the total revenue and marginal revenue equations
   for this demand curve.

c. What is the maximum total revenue obtainable if this
   is a firm's demand curve for X?

Word Problems Using Arc Elasticity (ref. EOCP 2; 4 through 11).

5. Rolf's Supermarkets now sell 12,000 lbs. of grapefruit
    per week at a price of $0.45 per lb. An economist has
    reported to management that the arc elasticity of demand
    for the grapefruit over the price range $0.45 to $0.35
    per lb. is -2.0. If Rolf's lowers its grapefruit price
    to $0.35 per lb., determine:

    a. how many grapefruit it will sell per week;

$$-2 = \frac{Q_2 - 12,000}{.35 - .45} \cdot \frac{.35 + .45}{Q_2 + 12,000}$$

$$-2Q_2 - 24,000 = (Q_2 - 12,000)(-8)$$
$$-2Q_2 - 24,000 = -8Q_2 + 96,000$$
$$-120,000 = -6Q_2$$
$$20,000 = Q_2$$

    b. how much its total revenue (TR) from grapefruit sales
       will increase.

$$TR = P \cdot Q = 12,000 \cdot (.45) = \$5,400 \qquad \$1,600$$
$$P_2 \cdot Q_2 = 20,000 \cdot .35 = \$7,000$$

           Getting Started:
                Set up the arc elasticity formula with Q_2
                as your unknown, and solve for the new
                quantity. Then compare the total revenue

after the price change with the initial TR. Since the absolute value of elasticity is greater than 1.0, TR should increase.

6. Pamela's Pizza Parlor has been considering a price reduction on its giant size Super Thick Crust Deep Pan Sicilian Style Pizza ("Sicilian" for short). Currently, the Sicilian is selling for an average price (three toppings) of $8.40. Pamela has hired an economic consultant, Vito Jones, to help her make the pricing decision. Vito (Jonesey for short) has estimated that the arc price elasticity for the Sicilian is about equal to -1.5 in the range being considered for the price change. Pamela's has been selling 1,200 Sicilian pizzas per week at the $8.40 price. To increase market share, Pamela would like to sell 2,000 per week.

Pamela also sells regular (thin crust) pizzas at an average price of $6.00 each. Currently, sales of regular pizzas have been 2,400 per week.

Given the information above, find the following:

a. The price Pamela would have to charge for the Sicilian pizzas in order to increase their sales quantity to 2,000 per week.

$$-1.5 = \frac{2000 - 1200}{P_2 - 8.40} \cdot \frac{P_2 + 8.40}{2000 + 1200}$$

$$\frac{800}{P_2 - 8.4} \cdot \frac{P_2 + 8.40}{3200}$$

$$-1.5p + 12.6 = P_2 + 2.1$$
$$-.25$$

$$10.5 = 1.75p$$

$$\$6.00 = P$$

b. The change in weekly total revenue from sales of Sicilian pizzas that accompanies the price change.

$$12,000 - 10,080 = 2000$$
$$1920$$

c. The amount of regular (thin crust) pizzas Pamela will sell after the above price cut in Sicilians, if the relevant cross elasticity is +1.20 and there is no change in the average price of the regular pizzas.

Getting Started:
As in the preceding problem, set up the arc elasticity formula, but this time with P_2 as the unknown. After solving for P_2, compare TR before and after the price change. Again, you should expect an increase in TR, since $|E| > 1$.

For part (c) use cross elasticity to find the new quantity of regular pizzas, given their initial quantity and the change in the price of Sicilian pizzas.

THE FOLLOWING PROBLEMS REQUIRE CALCULUS.

Demand Function Problems (ref. EOCP C2, C4, C5, C6, C7, C8).

7. Suppose a firm has calculated its demand function to be the following:

$$Q_x = 260 - 10P_x - 2P_y + .04I,$$

where Q_x is the weekly quantity demanded of good X, P_x is its own price, P_y is the price of a related good, and I is per capita annual income.

a. Assuming the price of Y is $200 and that per capita income is $12,000, write the equation of the demand <u>curve</u> for X. (The demand <u>function</u> is represented by the equation above.)

$$Q_x = 260 - 10P_x - 2(200) + .04(12,000)$$
$$Q_x = 260 - 10P_x - 400 + 480$$
$$Q_x = 340 - 10P_x$$

b. What is the point price elasticity of demand for X if the value of the independent variables above are P_X = $24, P_Y = $200, and I = $12,000?

$Q_x = 260 - 10(P_x) - 2P_y + .04I$ $Q_x = 340 - 10P_{(x)}$

$Q_x = 260 - 10(24) - 2(200) + .04(12,000)$

$E_p = \frac{dQ}{dx}\frac{P}{Q}$ $-10 \frac{24}{100} = -2.4$

c. Suppose P_X = $24. What is the arc cross elasticity of demand of X for changes in P_Y, over the range between the above price of Y and P_Y = $210? (Assume other independent variables keep the values above when the price of Y changes.) Are X and Y substitutes or complements? How do you know?

Getting Started:
Obtain Q_X by entering the given values of independent variables into the function. Then calculate elasticity. In (b), arc elasticity will require calculation of a second quantity for X.

To answer (c), recall that the demand curve will be of the form Q_X = a - $10P_X$, where a is the intercept term, a constant. Use the given values of the independent variables other than P_X to find a.

8. Pet 'n Gobble is a unique pet shop-restaurant combination where patrons can eat lunch or dinner while overlooking a pet store that sells small house pets. A consulting firm has estimated the following linear demand function for the pet sales portion of the business.

Q = 120 -2.0P -1.5P_d + 0.15M,

where

P = price of pets for sale
P_d = average price of dinners served in the restaurant
M = average monthly income of consumers in the area.

The current average income level in the area is $1,800 per month. The average price of a dinner served is $8.00, and the pets all sell for $100 each.

a. What are the current sales of pets and the total revenues from the pet business?

$$Q = 120 - 2(100) - 1.5(8.00) + .15(1800)$$
$$Q = 178$$

$$178 \cdot 100 = \$17,800$$

b. At the current quantity sold, what is the point price elasticity of demand for pets? Is demand elastic or inelastic?

$$-2 \cdot \frac{100}{178} = -1.12$$

Elastic

c. Does the equation indicate that pets and dinners are substitutes or that they are complements. <u>Explain</u>.

d. Below, calculate the income elasticity of pets given the current pet price, sales quantity, dinner price and income level.

$$.15 \frac{1800}{178} = 1.52$$

<u>Getting Started</u>:
    Use the given values of the independent
    variables to answer part (a). Then use
    the quantity you obtained to calculate

price elasticity.
Part (c) can be answered without an
elasticity calculation--note sign of
relevant variable. Income elasticity is,
of course, related to the coefficient of
the I variable.

Equation Using the Demand Curve (ref. EOCP C1, C3).

9. Suppose the demand curve for product X is:

$$Q_X = 4500 - 5P_X.$$

a. Below, write the equations of average revenue, total
revenue, and marginal revenue for this demand curve.

b. For the above data, at what quantity and price will total
revenue be maximized? How do you know?

c. How much will the dollar value of TR be at the maximum?

Getting Started:
Begin with the definition of each revenue
concept, and apply that to the given
curve. Recall what the value of MR will
be when TR is max to answer (b). Then
calculate the TR amount for the relevant
quantity.

MULTIPLE CHOICE
Circle the letter that corresponds to the best answer.

1. Texcolor Paints and Supplies lowered the price of its high
   quality paint from $20 to $18 per gallon for a special sale.
   As a result, the quantity sold per week increased, but weekly
   revenues from the sale of this paint decreased from $49,000 to
   $47,500. This information implies that for the exterior paint:
   (a) demand must be inelastic, since revenues fell;
   (b) the demand curve must be upward sloping;
   (c) the price elasticity of demand is positive, but only
       slightly so;
   (d) the arc price elasticity of demand over this range
       cannot be less than one.

2. For a straight-line, downward-sloping demand curve, when MR is
   zero, AR is:
   (a) at its midpoint value;
   (b) at a minimum;
   (c) increasing;
   (d) none of the above.

3. If a firm's total revenue is rising as it cuts the price of
   its product, we can reasonably expect that:
   (a) there are no good substitutes for the product;
   (b) the absolute value of its elasticity coefficient is
       greater than 1.0 in this range;
   (c) marginal revenue is rising in this range;
   (d) demand is inelastic in this range.

4. If the arc cross elasticity of demand between Product A and
   Product B is -3.56, we can readily conclude that:
   (a) the quantity sold of Product B will not respond much
       to a change in the price of Product A;
   (b) no one will buy Product A if Product B's price rises;
   (c) a price rise in Product B will lead to a decline in
       purchases of Product A;
   (d) someone has made an error since cross elasticity cannot
       be negative.

5. When a firm's demand curve is downward sloping, marginal
   revenue is generally:
   (a) less than price;
   (b) constant;
   (c) equal to price;
   (d) greater than price.

6. When TR is at a maximum, MR is:
   (a) at a maximum;
   (b) at a minimum;
   (c) increasing;
   (d) none of the above.

Chapter 2.

HAND-IN PROBLEMS

Name_____

Course No. and Section_____

Problem 1.

a. Suppose the equation of the firm's demand curve is

_____. Fill in the price column in the
(instructor supplied equation)
table below, and then complete the other two columns.

Quantity Sold	Price	Total Revenue	Marginal Revenue
0			
5			
10			
15			
20			
25			
30			

b. Calculate the arc elasticity of demand between quantity
sold = 20 and quantity sold = 25.

Chapter 2.

HAND-IN PROBLEMS

Name_____

Course No. & Section

Problem 2.

Grand Performance haircut company has hired a consultant to estimate the cross elasticity of demand between its haircuts and those offered by a major rival, Shear Magic. At present, Grand Performance is charging $9.00 for its regular cut, while Shear Magic is charging $10.00. The consultant estimates that within a range of $2.00 from Shear Magic's current price, the cross elasticity of demand for Grand Performance haircuts with respect to the price charged by Shear Magic is:

$$E_{gs} = \underline{\hspace{2cm}}.$$

(Instructor supplied number.)

Presently, Grand performance is selling _____ regular haircuts
(Instructor supplied number)
per week at its eight-dollar price. If the consultant is correct and Shear Magic cuts its price from $10.00 to $8.00 for a regular cut:

    a. What will be the sales quantity per week of Grand Performance's regular cuts, assuming they keep their price at $9.00?

    b. Calculate the change in Grand Performance's total revenue from regular cuts that follows from the above change.

Chapter 2.

HAND-IN PROBLEMS

Name_____

Course No. and Section_____

Problem 3.

ABC Company has estimated that the demand curve for its product is represented by the following equation:

$$Q = \underline{\hspace{2cm}} - 20P,$$ where Q is the quantity sold per week and P is the price per unit.

(Instructor supplied number.)

a. Based on the estimated demand curve, write the equations for ABC's:

   (1) Average Revenue;

   (2) Total Revenue;

   (3) Marginal Revenue.

b. What will be the maximum total revenue per week that ABC can obtain from sales of its product? (Give the exact dollar amount and explain how you determine it.)

c. Calculate the point price elasticity of demand for ABC's product when Q = 600. Is demand elastic or inelastic at this quantity? How do you know?

Chapter 2.

HAND-IN PROBLEMS

Name_____

Course No. and Section_____

THIS PROBLEM REQUIRES CALCULUS

<u>Problem 4.</u>

XYZ Corp., the world's largest seller of product X, has estimated its weekly demand for X to be given by the following equation:

$$Q_X = \underline{\hspace{2cm}} - 2.5P_X - 100P_y + 4P_z + .02I, \text{ where}$$

**(Instructor
 supplied number.)**

Q_X is units of X sold per week,
P_X is the price per unit of X,
P_y is the price per unit of Y,
P_z is the price per unit of Z,
I is per capita income of X purchasers.

Suppose at the present time that P_X = \$100, P_y = \$20, P_z = \$125, and I = \$10,000. Answer the following:

a. What is the equation of the demand curve for product X, assuming the values of the variables other than P_X remain as stated above?

b. Given your demand curve equation, what price and quantity will maximize revenue from sales of X, and what will the maximum possible weekly sales revenue be?

c. How is product Y related to product X? <u>Explain</u>. Calculate the point cross price elasticity of demand of product X for changes in the price of product Y, given the above-stated values of all independent variables.

CHAPTER 3: Demand Analysis and Estimation

Programmed Review

Chapter three looks at some basic topics in the area of demand estimation. The more closely a firm can estimate the _____ for its product, the more closely it can determine the price and level of output that will allow it to _____ its _____.

demand

maximize
profit

A firm may employ market surveys and market experiments to estimate the demand for its product. Often, managers can place more confidence in the results of a well-designed and executed market _____ than in the results of a market _____, since the former indicates how consumers actually reacted to certain changes rather than how they think they would react.

survey
experiment

_____ analysis is a statistical technique used to estimate the relationship between a dependent variable and a set of independent variables. In demand studies, usually the _____ variable is the quantity of some product sold per unit of time. The _____ variables usually include such things as the price of the product, the prices of related goods, and consumer incomes. If there is more than one independent variable, this statistical technique is called _____ regression. A measure of how closely the independent variables as a group are correlated with the dependent variable is given by ____, which is called the coefficient of _____. Three examples of regression studies of demand were cited in the chapter. Chow estimated the demand for _____, while Harp and Miller looked at the demand for a new

Regression

dependent
independent

multiple

R^2
determination

automobiles

_____ food.   Wilson estimated a demand   <u>convenience</u>
function for _____.   <u>electricity</u>

PRACTICE PROBLEMS

Problems on Estimated Demand Functions (ref. EOCQ 5, 6)

1. ARF Corp., the world's largest seller of product X, has estimated a demand function for X with the following results:

$$Q_X = 800 - 2.5P_X - 50P_Y + 4P_Z + .01I, \text{ where}$$

Q_X is units of X sold per week,
P_X is the price per unit of X,
P_Y is the price per unit of Y,
P_Z is the price per unit of Z,
I is per capita income of X purchasers.

$R^2 = 0.89$

a. Interpret the equation above with respect to the meaning of each estimated coefficient and discuss the meaning of R^2.

b. Suppose at the present time that P_X = $100, P_Y = $20, P_Z = $125, and I = $10,000. Answer the following:

  i)   What is the equation of the demand curve for product X, assuming the values of the variables other than P_X remain as stated above?

  ii) Given your demand curve equation, what price and quantity will maximize revenue from sales of X, and what will the maximum possible weekly sales revenue be?

iii)   Calculate the <u>own</u> point <u>price</u> elasticity of demand
       for X, given the stated values of the independent
       variables. (Elasticity of Q_X with respect to X's
       own price.)

2. Harry's Hot Old Fashioned Hamburgers has estimated the following demand curve for its top of the line burger, the McWhopperjaw:

$$Q_{mwj} = 2,000P_{mwj}^{-2.5}P_g^{4.2}P_c^{0.8}I^{-0.1}$$

where Q_{mwj} is the quantity sold of McWhopperjaws per day at a given location, P_g is the price of a competitor's major product, the Gagburger, P_c is the price of corn meal mush, and I is weekly consumer income.

a. How many McWhopperjaws will Harry's sell at the location if their price is $1.50, while that of Gagburgers is $1.35, that of corn meal mush is $0.50, and weekly income is $400?

b. Discuss the elasticity of the quantity sold of McWhopperjaws with respect to each of the independent variables in the demand function.

MULTIPLE CHOICE
Circle the letter that corresponds to the best answer.

1.   The statistic that indicates the proportion of the variation
     in the independent variable that is "explained" by a
     regression model is the:
     (a)   coefficient of determination;
     (b)   elasticity coefficient;
     (c) Y^2 coefficient;
     (d)   intercept coefficient.

2.   Suppose an estimated demand function is linear in logarithms.
     Then the elasticity of quantity with respect to any <u>one</u> of its
     independent variables will be:
     (a)   equal to 1.0;
     (b)   always greater than 1.0;
     (c)   a constant;
     (d)   incalculable.

3.   Gregory Chow's well-known regression analysis of the
     demand for automobiles lends support to the hypothesis that:
     (a)   the income elasticity for car ownership is greater than
           the price elasticity for the same;
     (b)   a decline in the demand for automobiles in the United
           States is the major cause of world recessions;
     (c)   advertising is the most important independent variable
           in the demand function for automobiles;
     (d)   manufacturers' rebate programs occur frequently because
           of the high price elasticity of demand for automobiles.

4.   The reason market experiments tend to be more reliable than
     market surveys is:
     (a)   experiments are usually more carefully constructed than
           are survey instruments;
     (b)   experiments reveal what people actually do, rather than
           what they say they will do;
     (c)   firms requesting surveys usually request a biased form
           of survey instrument;
     (d)   researchers engaged in conducting market experiments
           are usually better trained than those who design
           surveys.

Chapter 3.

HAND-IN PROBLEMS

Name_____

Course No. and Section_____

Problem 1.

ARF Corporation has determined that the elasticity of demand for

its product is _____.   If the average variable cost of the
             (instructor supplied number)

product is constant at AVC = 5.00, what is the firm's profit-
maximizing price?

Chapter 3.

HAND-IN PROBLEMS

Name_____

Course No. and Section_____

Problem 2.

The management of <u>Just Folks</u> magazine has asked its economic analysis department to examine the demand for <u>Just Folks</u> in cities of 80,000 to 100,000 population. The department chose a cross section of 50 cities to analyze for the month of September. The variables it considered were the price of <u>Just Folks</u> (P_f), that of <u>Ordinary People</u> (P_O), another popular magazine, the price of the <u>National Review</u> (P_r), <u>Just Folks</u>' advertising (A), and per capita income (I). The following demand function was estimated by least squares:

$$Q_f = \underline{\hspace{2cm}} - 2{,}500P_f - 1{,}200P_O + 2{,}400P_r + 4A + .25I$$
$$\textbf{(instructor supplied number)}$$

(Q_f is the weekly quantity sold in one city.)

The regression program also yielded the following result.

$$R^2 = 0.92$$

a. What does the R^2 of 0.92 mean?

b. Suppose that <u>Just Folks</u> sells for $2.25, while the price of <u>Ordinary People</u> is $2.45. At the same time, the <u>National Review</u> is priced at $3.25. If <u>Just Folks</u> spends $8,000 on advertising in a given city in this size class with a per capita income of $12,000, how many magazines can it expect to sell per week? What will be the own price elasticity of demand for <u>Just Folks</u> in such a market? Calculate also the relevant cross price elasticities, the advertising elasticity, and the income elasticity of demand. (Show work.)

(continued next page)

(Ch. 3, H-I Problem 2, continued)

c. Now, suppose <u>Just Folks</u> has a constant unit variable cost of $0.10 per copy to produce the magazine. Assuming the values of P_o, P_r, A, and I given above, what will be the firm's profit-maximizing combination of price and quantity sold in a typical town of 80,000 to 100,000 population?

CHAPTER 4: Economic Forecasting

Programmed Review

This chapter deals with the issue of economic forecasting. Forecasting is the process of analyzing available information regarding economic variables and relationships and then predicting the future values of certain variables.

Forecasts are frequently made regarding aggregate macroeconomic variables. For example, the final market value of goods and services produced in a country during some time period is called _____ domestic _____ . Purchases of new plant, equipment, and inventories by businesses and purchases of new residential housing are _____ spending, while spending by individuals for newly produced goods and services is called _____ expenditures. Expenditures for goods and services by state and local governments and the federal government are reported as _____ expenditures. The value of newly produced U.S. goods and services purchased by foreigners (exports) less the value of newly produced foreign goods purchased by the United States (imports) is defined as our ____ _____.

<u>gross</u>   <u>product</u>

<u>investment</u>

<u>consumption</u>

<u>government</u>

<u>net</u>
<u>exports</u>

Two general types of data are used by forecasters. Observations regarding a specific variable over a number of time periods are _____ _____ data. Observations regarding a particular variable at a single point in time are _____ _____ data.

<u>time</u>
<u>series</u>

<u>cross</u> <u>section</u>

The factors that affect the values of economic variables can be classified into the following four general categories: _____, seasonal, _____, and _____. Trend factors are

<u>trend</u>

<u>cyclical</u>   <u>other</u>

47

those which reflect movements in economic variables over time. Factors that are related to a
specific time of the year are called _____   seasonal
factors. Factors that are related to fluctuations
in the general level of business activity are
called _____ factors.   cyclical

     Five types of forecasting techniques are
discussed this chapter. They are econometric
models, barometric forecasting, surveys, trend
analysis, and ARIMA models. Two methods that
rely primarily on historical data to predict the
future are _____ _____ and ARIMA mod-   trend analysis
els. The method that uses current values of certain economic variables called indicators to
predict the future values of other economic variables is called _____ forcasting. A   barometric
forecasting tool that uses the techniques of regression analysis is that called _____   econometric
modelling. Equations that describe how the values of one or more economic variables are related
to the value of some other economic variable are
_____ equations. Equations that must   behavioral
be true by definition are called _____.   identities

MULTIPLE CHOICE
Circle the letter that corresponds to the best answer.

1. The two major types of data used by economic forecasters are:
   (a)   real data and imaginary data;
   (b)   financial data and physical data;
   (c)   GNP data and foreign trade data;
   (d)   time series data and cross-section data.

2. The part of a business cycle that follows its trough is its phase of:
   (a)   expansion;
   (b)   stagnation;
   (c)   contraction;
   (d)   repercussion.

3. Barometric forecasting in economics makes use of:
   (a)   climatological maps;
   (b)   mercurial forecasting equipment;
   (c)   weathermen;
   (d)   leading indicators.

4. In barometric economic forecasts, a <u>diffusion index</u> indicates:
   (a)   what percentages of leading indicators are rising in value;
   (b)   the degree to which economic experts disagree about expansion vs. contraction;
   (c)   the percentage of jobs in the economy that will be affected by a recession;
   (d)   whether the stock market is moving in coordination with other economic variables.

5. The two types of equations common to all econometric models are:
   (a)   difference equations and differential equations;
   (b)   behavioral equations and identities;
   (c)   specific equations and general equations;
   (d)   concrete equations and speculative equations.

CHAPTER 5: Production Analysis

Programmed Review

The objective of this chapter is to develop
some economic principles of production that can
be widely applied to the activities of firms as
well as agencies of government. In the case of
the firm, we assume that the objective is to
maximize _____, and we note that to do this   <u>profit</u>
it is necessary also to minimize _____ of pro-   <u>cost</u>
duction. We begin with a mathematical statement
that spells out the recipe that the firm must
use if it is to minimize its cost of production.
This statement is the _____ function, and   <u>production</u>
it is viewed as showing all of the combinations
of inputs that can produce various possible levels
of output of some good or service, given the ex-
isting state of _____.   <u>technology</u>

To discuss production, it is convenient to define two time periods, the long run and the short
run. In the long run, all inputs of the produc-
tion function are _____, but in the short   <u>variable</u>
run at least one input is _____. A two-input   <u>fixed</u>
production function can be used to develop the
principles of production in a simplified form.
Such a function can be reduced to a two-dimension-
al graph using contour lines, known in economics
as _____, to describe each level of output   <u>isoquants</u>
in terms of the various combinations of inputs
that can be used to produce it. A single produc-
tion isoquant shows only _____ level of output.   <u>one</u>

Isoquants are generally bowed toward the ori-
gin because the marginal rate of _____   <u>substitution</u>
diminishes as the firm attempts to substitute
one input for another. This happens since inputs
frequently are not perfect _____ for one   <u>substitutes</u>

51

another. Thus, it becomes increasingly difficult
to use one in place of the other as successive
substitutions are made.

It is possible to draw a line in the isoquant
diagram that represents all of the combinations
of two inputs that can be purchased with a given
budget at <u>given</u> input prices. This is called
the _____ line. Tangency between this line   <u>isocost</u>
and an isoquant will identify the least cost in-
put combination for the level of output on that
isoquant. At such a point it will be true that
a dollar spent on either of the two inputs has
the _____ marginal effect on output.   <u>same</u>

Passing isocost lines for successively larger
budgets through the isoquant diagram generates a
path of least-cost points which is known as the
_____ path. It is from the this path that   <u>expansion</u>
we obtain data on the firm's long run total and
per unit costs. The behavior of unit costs will
depend on what kind of _____ to scale the   <u>returns</u>
production function exhibits; increasing, cons-
tant, or decreasing.

In the short run the firm is operating from
a given size plant; thus some of the firm's
inputs are fixed. The short-run _____   <u>product</u>
curves describe this situation. Total output is
shown on the _____ _____ curve, and its   <u>total</u> <u>product</u>
rate of change is shown by the _____ prod-   <u>marginal</u>
uct curve. The last relevant product curve for
the short run is _____ product, which is   <u>average</u>
obtained by dividing total product by the number
of units employed of the _____ input.   <u>variable</u>

The concept that measures the revenue generated by employing an additional unit of a given

input is usually called the marginal _____   revenue
_____ of that input. A firm will use more   product
of a short-run variable input as long as its MRP
exceeds the additional cost to the firm of obtaining the input.

PRACTICE PROBLEMS

Problems on Long-Run Least Cost Combination of Inputs
(ref. EOCP 1, 3, 5, 7, 8, 11)

1. Joe's Parking Lot Service is evaluating its current
    operations to determine whether it should invest in a
    new paint-striping machine or some additional stencils
    to add to its parking-lot striping capacity. The new
    stencils would cost $24 each. The paint striping machine
    would cost $450. Currently, Joe estimates that with each
    additional stencil his crew can stripe 6 more parking
    spaces per hour. The striping machine can paint 150
    parking spaces per hour. Should Joe choose to buy addi-
    tional stencils or the machine? Why? Would the amount
    of additional business anticipated affect his decision?
    Explain.

Getting Started:
    For both this problem and the following
    two you must first determine the marginal
    product of each input. Then relate it to
    the price of the input in accordance with
    the least-cost rule.

2. La Venganza Tortilla Company is trying to determine whether or not to install a fully automated tortilla press. Currently they use twenty workers and twenty hand presses to form the tortillas. The cost per hour for one worker is $4.00. Since a tortilla craze has hit the country, La Venganza's business is booming, and the firm needs to expand its output. The firm can increase its output by 1000 tortillas per hour if it adds one worker and purchases a tortilla machine. One additional worker with a hand press can produce 200 tortillas per hour. The estimated cost per year (depreciation, interest charges, maintenance, electricity, etc.), for an automated press is $6,000, based on a working year of 260 eight-hour days. The cost per hour for one hand press is $.01.
    What is the cheapest way for La Venganza to expand its output? Why?

3. A firm that installs lawn sprinkler systems has found that with one additional jackhammer it can lay an average of 400 additional feet of sprinkler pipe per day. One additional worker can lay an additional 20 feet of pipe per hour. Each worker will cost the firm $18 per hour, and a jackhammer will cost $196 per day. Assuming an eight-hour workday, which method should the firm use to expand its level of output? Why?

4. Given the following production data for a firm:

Units of Input b	Output of Product X					
6	122	205	277	345	408	468
5	112	190	256	317	374	429
4	100	168	228	283	334	383
3	86	145	197	245	289	331
2	70	119	160	200	236	270
1	50	84	114	142	167	191
	1	2	3	4	5	6

Units of Input a

a. Calculate the average and marginal product of input a as its use varies from one to 6 units, given that input b is fixed at b = 3 units.

b. Calculate the average and marginal product of input b as its use varies from one to 6 units, given that input a is fixed at a = 2 units.

c. If the price of a unit of input a is $40 and that of one unit of input b is $42, is b = 3, a = 2 a least

cost combination of inputs for an output of 145
units of product X?   Explain.

d. What kind of returns to scale are given by the data
in the table?   How do you know?

Getting Started:
Use the definitions of AP and MP to
calculate your per unit values in (a) and
(b).   You might want to make a table with
columns for a, Q_x, AP_a, and MP_a when b is
fixed, and likewise for b when a is
fixed.   Apply the least cost rule to
answer part (c).   Change inputs
proportionally to test for returns to
scale.

Problems on Short-Run Product of a Variable Input
(ref. EOCP 2, 6, 9)

5.   Given the following short-run total product curve for
the single variable input L:

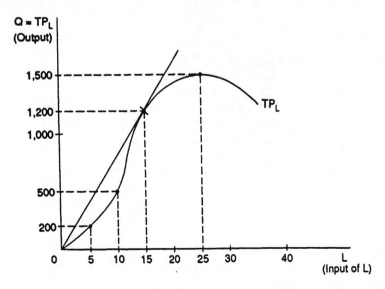

a. What is the average product of L when 500 units of output are produced?

b. At what level of L use will AP_L be maximum?

c. Calculate the value of MP_L for each of the given changes in L use as L varies from L = 0 to L = 25.

d. Briefly explain how MP_L is related to AP_L, using the numbers above in your explanation.

Getting Started:
Use AP_L definition to perform calculation for it; likewise for MP_L. Ray from origin has specific relation to both per unit curves. Apply average-marginal relationship in (d).

6. Complete the following table. Assume that z is the variable input and that all other inputs are fixed in the short run.

Units of z	TP_z	AP_z	MP_z
0	0	---	
			100
2	200	100	
			200
4	600	150	
			150
6	900	150	
			102
8	1104	138	
			73
10	1250	125	

Getting Started:
Definitions of the various product concepts are important in filling in the preceding table. In the case of arc marginal product, if you multiply the change in z times the marginal product of an additional unit of z, you can determine the change in total product. Try to fill in the total product column first.

THE FOLLOWING PROBLEM REQUIRES CALCULUS

Relation of Short-Run Total Product Function to Per Unit Product Functions   (ref. EOCP C1, C2, C3, C4, C5, C6, C7)

7. Suppose the total product of labor curve for the XYZ Company is given by the following equation, where Q is output and L is the number of workers employed:

$$Q = 45L + 6L^2 - \frac{1}{3}L^3$$

a. Write the equation for the marginal product of labor.

b. Write the equation for the average product of labor.

c. What is the maximum total output (Q) obtainable by this firm, assuming we are in the short run and that labor is the only variable input.

d. At what level of labor input will marginal product of labor be maximum?

e. What will be the maximum value of average product of labor?   (How many units of output per worker?)

<u>Getting Started</u>:
Use the calculus definition of MP_L in part (a). AP_L can be obtained from its algebraic definition. Maximum output occurs when $MP_L = 0$. The extreme values of MP_L and AP_L occur where their respective derivatives are zero.

MULTIPLE CHOICE
Circle the letter that corresponds to the best answer.

1. In an isoquant diagram, which of the following will lead to a change in the MRTS between two inputs;
    (a) a movement along an isoquant;
    (b) a change in the firm's budget;
    (c) a proportional change in input prices;
    (d) none of the above.

2. Which of the following statements concerning the short-run product curves for a variable input is correct?
    (a) the marginal passes through the average when the average is maximum;
    (b) the marginal product curve can never become negative;
    (c) the average product curve can become negative;
    (d) when the total product is maximum, the average product is zero.

3. The slope of an isocost line is equal to:
    (a) the MRTS;
    (b) the ratio of the marginal revenues of the two inputs;
    (c) the ratio of the prices of the two inputs;
    (d) the price of one input times that of the other.

4. At the point of diminishing marginal returns on a short-run total product curve, the AP of the variable input is:
    (a) at a maximum;
    (b) at a minimum;
    (c) equal to zero;
    (d) none of the above.

5. In the long run, all inputs are;
    (a) implicit;
    (b) variable;
    (c) fixed;
    (d) equal in terms of marginal product.

Chapter 5.

HAND-IN PROBLEMS

Name_____

Course No. and Section_____

Problem 1.

Given:

Units of K	Estimated Output						
6	461	654	800	924	1033	1128	
5	421	597	731	843	940	1033	
4	376	534	653	752	843	924	
3	327	462	564	652	731	800	
2	267	376	462	534	597	654	
1	188	267	327	376	421	461	
	1	2	3	4	5	6	Units of L

(continued next page)

(Prob. 1, continued)

   a. Complete the table below, assuming that the physical

      amount of capital is fixed at _____ units.
                    (instructor supplied
                        number)

Units of L	TP_L	AP_L	MP_L
1			
2			
3			
4			
5			
6			

   b. As more and more capital is combined with a given
      amount of labor, what happens to MP_L? Why?
      Give an example from the original table.

(continued next page)

(Chapter 5, Prob. 1, continued)

c. Does this production function appear to have
   constant, increasing, or decreasing returns to scale?
   Why? Give an example from the original table.

d. If P_K = $150 and P_L = $120, is K = 4 and L = 3 a
   least cost combination of inputs? Why or why not?

e. Is the use of a least cost combination of inputs
   necessary for long-run profit maximization? Is it
   sufficient to ensure that profit is maximized? Why
   or why not?

Chapter 5.

HAND-IN PROBLEMS

Name_____

Course No. and Section_____

Problem 2.

A local letter shop is currently using a combination of computer-based word processors and electronic memory typewriters to produce form letters and pamphlets for its clients. A consultant has been retained to see whether costs can be reduced through some realignment of equipment. The consultant finds that the shop could produce an additional 264 pages of text per day with eight more word processors and 300 pages per day from 10 more electronic typewriters.

The shop leases both types of machines from well-known, competitive leasing firms. Currently, it is paying $110 per

month for the word processors and $_____ per month for the
                                    **(instructor supplied
                                          number)**

electronic memory typewriters. (The letter shop bases its operations on 22 working days per month.)

   a. Should the letter shop consider changing its mix
      of word processors and electronic typewriters?

   b. Explain why you conclude the above.

Chapter 5.

HAND-IN PROBLEMS

Name_____

Course No. and Section_____

Problem 3.   (REQUIRES CALCULUS)

R Company has the following production function where Q is output, K is the amount of physical capital employed, and L is the number of units of labor hired. Suppose the firm is in the short run with capital fixed at K =

_____.

(instructor supplied number)

$$Q = 27KL + 4KL^2 - \frac{1}{9}KL^3$$

(Show all calculations.)

   a.   At what L value will the MP_L for this firm equal zero?

   b.   What will be the maximum short-run output the firm can produce?

   c.   What will be the numerical value of MP_L at its maximum?

   d.   What will be the numerical value of AP_L when it is at its maximum?

CHAPTER 6: Cost of Production

Programmed Review

In order to maximize profit a firm must obtain the largest spread possible between its total revenue from sales and its total cost of production.   Of course, this requires that the firm produce its output at the _____ possible total cost.

least

There are several types of costs that the firm must consider. Costs that appear on ordinary income statements prepared by accountants are called _____ costs or historical costs. These are only a part of the economic costs of the firm. The economic cost of production includes both explicit costs and _____ costs. The latter are the costs of using resources the firm owns in a given way instead of in their next-best use. Foregone interest on funds invested in a firm, instead of elsewhere, is an example of an _____ cost. To accurately describe the economic costs of the firm, both explicit and implicit costs are included in the cost functions and curves used by economists.

explicit

implicit

implicit

Long run economic costs are based on the long-run analysis of production, where the firm has no fixed inputs.   It follows that all costs are _____ in the long run. The data on long-run output are the source of the data on long-run cost.

variable

Long-run average cost may remain constant, fall, or rise depending on the type of _____ to _____ exhibited by the firm's production function. If returns to scale are constant, long-run average cost will be _____. Increasing

returns

scale

constant

returns to scale yield _____ long-run average   <u>falling</u>
cost, while decreasing returns yield _____ long-   <u>rising</u>
run average cost.

In the short run, some costs are variable
while others are _____. The firm's short run   <u>fixed</u>
cost curves are closely related to its short-run
_____ curves. Total variable cost rises as   <u>product</u>
output increases, its rate of change being depen-
dent on the behavior of the _____ product of   <u>marginal</u>
variable inputs. The rate of change of total
cost (or total variable cost) as output changes
is called _____ _____. Because of diminish-   <u>marginal</u> <u>cost</u>
ing returns to variable inputs in the short run,
marginal cost can be expected to eventually ___   <u>rise</u>
as output increases.

The curve of average fixed cost always ____   <u>falls</u>
as quantity produced increases. However, average
variable cost and short-run average cost are both
U-shaped curves if the firm has first increasing
but later diminishing marginal product. Both AVC
and SAC will be intersected at their respective
minimum points by the rising portion of the
_____ cost curve.   <u>marginal</u>

Long-run and short-run costs are related. For
example, the long-run average cost curve is an
_____ curve made up of relevant points on   <u>envelope</u>
the firm's many possible short-run average cost
curves. When the firm chooses its best input
combination for the long run, it identifies a
size of _____ consistent with some set of cost   <u>plant</u>
data for short-run operations. Whether in the
short or the long run, the firm must minimize
cost if it is to attain its objective of maximum
_____.   <u>profit</u>

PRACTICE PROBLEMS

Tabular Problems on Cost of Production
    (ref. EOCP 1, 2, 4, 5, 7, 8, 9, 10, 11)

1. Complete the following table, given that L is labor units, Q is units of output, and that P_L, the price of a unit of labor is fixed. Assume that L is the only variable input.

MP	L	Q	STC	AFC	AVC	TVC	MC
	0	0	200	---	---	0	
	5	20		10		250	
	10	60					
	15	90				750	
	20	110					
	25	125					
	30	135					
	35	140					

Getting Started:
    First fill in your marginal product values. From the figures in the table you can determine the price of input L and then generate the remaining data. If you are unsure about the definitions of any of the cost concepts, look them up in the chapter or refer to the glossary at the end of the book.

2. The following data represent the outputs of product X that can be obtained from various combinations of two inputs, a, and b.

Units of Input b	Output of Product X					
6	24	35	42	49	55	60
5	22	32	39	45	50	55
4	20	28	35	40	45	49
3	17	24	30	35	39	42
2	14	20	24	28	32	35
1	10	14	17	20	22	24
	1	2	3	4	5	6

Units of Input a

Suppose the price of a unit of input a is $40, while that of a unit of input b is $30. Given that input a is fixed at a = 3, complete the table below.

SMC	MP_b	Output of X	Input of b	AP_b	AVC	STC
		0	0			

Getting Started;
   Remember that input a is fixed at 3 and that the relevant production data are those generated as b varies. Since you have the price per unit for each of these, you can easily determine total fixed cost and total variable cost.

Relation of Expansion Path to Long-Run Average Cost   (ref. EOCP 3)

3. Given the following diagram:

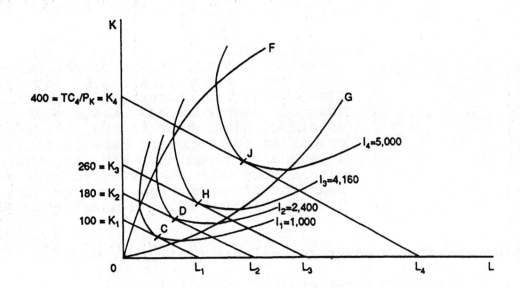

a) In the quadrant below, sketch the long-run average cost curve, assuming that the price of a unit of capital is P_K = $80 and the price of a unit of labor is P_L = $60.

b) Determine the numerical value of the marginal rate of technical substitution at the point of cost minimization on each of isoquants in the given diagram.

c) Explain how long-run marginal cost is related to the long-run average cost curve you have drawn.

Getting Started:
Remember that the amount of the budget along any isocost line can be determined from the maximum amount of either input that can be purchased. Also, there is a specific relation of the MRTS to the input prices at any tangency between an isocost line and an isoquant. Finally, there is also a very specific relation between the behavior of an average curve and the location of its related marginal curve.

Relation of Total Product to Variable Cost (ref. EOCP 6)

4.   Given the total product curve below:

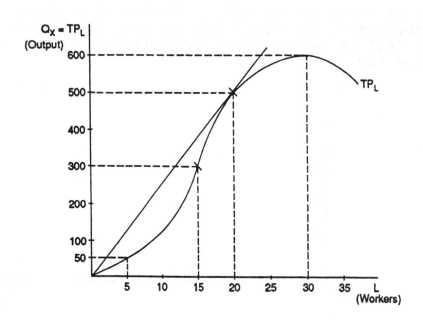

Assume that P_L, the price of a worker, is $40.

Fill in the blanks:

a) The marginal product of labor will equal zero when the number of workers employed equals _____.

b) Average variable cost and marginal cost will be equal
   when output is _____ units.

c) The minimum value of AVC is $_____ per unit.

d) When total product is 300, average product equals _____.
   When total product is 600, average product is _____.

e) If the firm produces 500 units of output with total fixed
   cost of $450, its total cost will be $_____, and its
   short-run average cost will be $_____.

<u>Getting Started:</u>
This problem relies on the definitions of
the various product and cost concepts. If
you keep them in mind, you will find that
you have enough information to fill in all
the blanks.

THE FOLLOWING PROBLEMS REQUIRE CALCULUS

Relation of Short-Run Total Cost to Per Unit Functions (ref. EOCP C1, C2, C3, C4, C5, C6, C7)

5. Given the following short-run total cost function:

   $$TC = 2{,}000 + 40Q - 0.5Q^2 + .02Q^3 ,$$ where Q is units of output.

   Write equations for:

   a) AVC

   b) SMC

   c) AFC

   d) SAC

   Find:

   e) SAC when output = 20 units

f) AFC when output = 40 units

g) the output corresponding to minimum AVC.

Getting Started:
    Definitions again are important here.
    Note that 2,000 is the only fixed term in
    the TC function and therefore represents
    TFC. The variable cost items will be
    derived from the rest of the function. To
    get marginal cost, you will have to
    differentiate the function. To find
    minimum AVC, you will have to set a
    derivative equal to zero.

6. Suppose a firm has the following short-run total cost
   function:

$$STC = 500 + 40Q - 1.5Q^2 + 0.04Q^3,$$

   where Q is output.

Answer the following:

a) What is the dollar value of average fixed cost at an
output of 20 units?

b) At what level of output will marginal cost be minimum?

c) What will be the value of average variable cost when it is minimum?

Getting Started:
   The procedure here is much the same as in the immediately preceding problem. Again, be sure you have defined the correct cost concept and that you set the appropriate derivative equal to zero when determining a minimum.

MULTIPLE CHOICE
Circle the letter that corresponds to the best answer.

1. Which of the following cost concepts relates most directly
    to the expansion path in an isoquant diagram?
    (a) implicit costs;
    (b) fixed costs;
    (c) long-run costs;
    (d) hidden costs.

2. If a production function is characterized by increasing
    returns to scale, long-run average cost will:
    (a) rise as output increases;
    (b) be constant;
    (c) show no evidence of economies of scale;
    (d) be a falling function of output.

3. Implicit costs can be thought of as the costs of:
    (a) dealing with unknown factors of production;
    (b) using resources owned by the firm in its own production
        process;
    (c) paying for the services of labor employed by the firm;
    (d) coping with government regulations.

4. The reason average fixed cost falls as quantity produced
    increases is that:
    (a) it is always cheaper to produce more than less;
    (b) the firm enjoys discounts on materials prices as it
        increases the amount of output it produces;
    (c) the firm enjoys economies of scale in the short run;
    (d) total fixed cost is spread over more and more units of
        product as output increases.

5. If the average product curve for a firm first rises and later
    falls as output is increased in the short run:
    (a) the firm's AVC curve will have a minimum point;
    (b) the TVC curve of the firm will eventually fall;
    (c) AVC and marginal cost will be the same at all output
        levels in the short run.;
    (d) the marginal product of the firm's variable inputs will
        always be greater than the average product of those same
        inputs.

Chapter 6.

HAND-IN PROBLEMS

Name_____

Course No. and Section_____

Problem 1.

Suppose a firm has two inputs, X and Y, and that Y is fixed in the short run. Its short-run total product is described by the following table.

X	Q = Output
0	0
2	20
4	100
6	132
8	160
10	180
12	192

Fill in the table below, assuming that the price of a unit of input

X is $_____,   that Y is fixed at Y = 10, and that the firm
       **(Instructor
        supplied number)**

must pay $_____ per unit for Y.
       **(instructor supplied
        number)**

SMC	MP$_X$	Output (Q)	Input of X	AP$_X$	AVC	STC

Chapter 6.

HAND-IN PROBLEMS

Name_____

Course No. and Section_____

Problem 2.

Given:

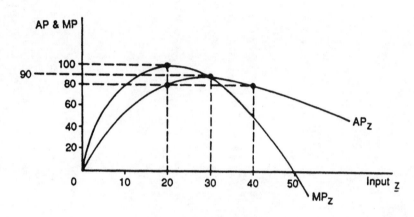

Suppose the firm is in the short run and input z is the only variable input. Further, P_z, the price of a unit of input z, is

$_____, and total fixed cost is $_____.
(instructor supplied   **(instructor supplied**
 number)   **number)**

a. How much is marginal cost when the firm is producing 1,600 units of output per week? (Express algebraically and give dollar amount.)

b. At what level of output will AVC = SMC? How do you know?

c. Calculate the value of AVC when z = 40. What other output level has the same AVC? How can you tell?

d. Calculate total cost (STC) when output = 2700. Explain how you did it.

Chapter 6.

HAND-IN PROBLEMS

Name_____

Course No. and Section_____

Problem 3.

Suppose a firm has the following total cost function:

$$TC = \underline{\hspace{5cm}},$$
$$\text{(Instructor supplied equation)}$$

where Q is
weekly output.

a) Write equations for:

i) Average Fixed Cost.

ii) Average Variable Cost.

b) What will be the value of short-run average cost
when Q = 60?   (Show work.)

c) What will average fixed cost be when Q = 20?

THE NEXT TWO ITEMS REQUIRE CALCULUS

d) Write the marginal cost equation for this firm.

e) For this firm, what will be the dollar value of AVC at
its minimum?   (Show work.)

CHAPTER 7: Profit Analysis of the Firm

Programmed Review

In this chapter, the materials on revenue and cost are brought together to describe maximization of profit by the firm. As in the preceding chapter, the firm's total cost will be viewed as including all costs of getting its product to market, both explicit and _____   implicit
costs. Thus, total economic profit will be the difference between total _____ and total cost.   revenue

If the firm has a downward sloping demand curve, it maximizes profit by selecting the right combination of quantity sold and _____ for its   price
product. Normally, reductions in price will cause quantity sold to _____, but this change can   increase
only be accomplished by also increasing costs. It will be desirable to make such a change as long as it adds more to _____ than it does   revenue
to total cost.

Total profit will be maximized when its rate of change, called _____ profit, is zero.   marginal
At this maximum, marginal _____ is equal   revenue
to marginal cost, and for greater quantities of output, marginal _____ will exceed marginal   cost
_____. If marginal revenue equals marginal   revenue
cost at a point where an increase in quantity sold results in MR > MC, that point will be the minimum of the total profit curve, rather than its maximum.

When using tabular data, the profit-maximizing output can be determined by comparing arc marginal revenue with _____ marginal _____ for each   arc   cost
increase in quantity. If for an increase in quantity sold, arc marginal revenue exceeds arc marginal cost, marginal profit will be _____,   positive

87

and total profit will _____. However, quan-   increase
tity sold should not be increased if the change
in _____ exceeds that in revenue.   In addition   cost
to profit-maximizing analysis, firms often use
breakeven analysis to relate quantity sold to
_____.   Breakeven analysis assumes that the   profit
firm is in the short run (TFC=0) and that both
price and average variable cost are _____.   constants
The difference between price and AVC is called
the _____ contribution _____.   This   profit margin
margin above AVC, when multiplied by quantity
sold, measures the firm's total _____ contri-   profit
bution.   Break-even occurs when the firm has sold
a large enough quantity to make (P-AVC) multiplied
by Q just equal its total _____ cost.   Any   fixed
quantity larger than the break-even quantity
yields a positive _____ for the firm. Breakeven   profit
analysis can roughly approximate profit maximizing
analysis if the firm considers expected break-even
points and expected levels of profit under different price, cost, and output alternatives.

Incremental profit analysis is a variant of
traditional profit _____ analysis that   maximizing
deals with the impact on the firm's total profit
of large, rather than marginal, changes in its
operations. In keeping with the outcome of profit
maximizing analysis, incremental profit analysis
shows that a change is worth considering if it
results in incremental _____ that exceed its   revenues
incremental _____.   costs

PRACTICE PROBLEMS

Tabular Problems on the Profit-Maximizing Level of Output
    (ref. EOCP 1, 3, 5, and 7)

1. The table below gives revenue and cost data for a manu-facturer of tennis shoes. All data are per pair of tennis shoes manufactured per minute.

Q	P	TR	MR	MC	Mπ	TVC
0	$30	$ 0	27	25	2	$ 0
1	27	27	24	20	4	25
3	25	75	20	14	4	65
5	23	115	19	10	9	97
10	21	210	15	15	0	147
12	20	240	10	18	-8	177
15	18	270	6	20	-14	231
20	15					331
26	12					463
39	8					775

a. Complete the table above.

b.   What are the firm's profit-maximizing price and output?

c.   If the firm's total fixed cost were $30 per minute, what is economic profit at the point given in (b)?

2.   The table below gives revenue and cost data for Estate Lighting, a company that makes dining room chandeliers.

Q	P	TR	MR	MC	Mπ	TVC	AFC
0	$800	$ 0		$400		$ 0	---
			$		$		
200	750			350			$
400	700			300			
600	650			300			
800	600			400			
1,000	550			500			60
1,200	500			600			
1,400	450						

a.   Complete the table above.

b. What are the profit-maximizing price and level of
    output for Estate Lighting? WHY?

3. Earth Forces, Inc., manufactures a durable toy light saber
    that sends out very bright rays of light when it is turned
    on. Some revenue and cost data for the firm's product
    are given in the table below.

TC=50 TFC=50
       TVC=0   ATR/ΔQ   MR-MC

Q	P	TR	MR	MC	Mπ	TVC	AFC
0	$50	$ 0	45	$20	75	$ 0	---
100	45	4,500	35	15	20		$
200	40	8,000	25	10	15	3500	15
300	35	10,500	15	5	10	4,500	
400	30	12,000	5				
500	25	12,500	-5			5,600	
600	20	12,000				6,600	

a. Fill in the blank boxes in the above table.

b. What will be this firm's profit-maximizing price and
    level of output? WHY?

c. Over what range of output and price does the price elasticity of demand become inelastic for Earth Forces? WHY? (Hint: You do not have to compute any additional figures after you have completed Part (a) to answer this question.)

Problems on Breakeven Analysis (ref. EOCP 2, 4, 6, 8, 9)

4. An electric motor manufacturing company has current plant capacity of one million motors per year. Unit variable costs associated with this plant are $10 and fixed costs are $1 million. It is estimated that the current capacity number of engines can be sold for $20 each. The firm is considering expanding its plant facilities so that the current capacity will be doubled. Under this proposal, unit variable costs would be expected to decrease to $5 and fixed cost to increase to $1.8 million. The firm estimates that it could sell 1.5 million units at a price of $15.

    a. Find the breakeven quantity with the current plant (price equals $20) and with the new plant (price equals $15).

    b. Find expected profit for each plant for the estimated sales (1 million units for the current plant at a price of $20, and 1.5 million units for the proposed plant at a price of $15).

5.   Appalachian Steel produces cold-rolled sheet steel. Cur-
     rently, the firm is producing and selling 9,000 tons of
     steel per year at a price of $400 per ton. Plant capacity
     is 10,000 tons per year. Average variable costs per ton
     are as follows:

        Direct Labor $90
        Direct Materials   80
        Variable Manufacturing overhead   50
        Variable Selling Expenses   30

Total fixed costs are $1,200,000.

     a.   Find the breakeven point for Appalachian Steel with
          the above plant.

     b.   Because of a target pricing policy on imported steel
          recently adopted by the U.S. government, Appalachian
          believes the demand for its steel will increase, so
          it is considering a plan to build an addition to its
          present plant that will increase capacity to 20,000
          units.   Total fixed costs will rise to $3,000,000.
          However, because of the increased efficiency of the
          new equipment, average variable manufacturing overhead
          costs are expected to fall to $20 per ton. Appalachian
          Steel believes it can sell 16,000 tons of steel at a
          price of $380 per ton.

          Would you recommend that Appalachian Steel build the
          plant addition? Why or why not? Show expected profit
          before and after plant expansion.

6. The income statement for a recent month for a 600 room hotel is given below:

Casa Rio Hotel
Income Statement
February, 198X

Sales (11,200 rooms @ $80) $896,000

Less Operating Expenses:

Laundry	$ 48,800	
Room Supplies	22,400	
Salaries and Wages	109,600	
Telephones	8,480	
Utilities	35,600	
Advertising	12,200	
Office Supplies	6,000	
Maintenance	40,320	
Dues	2,000	
Miscellaneous	22,400	$307,800

Gross Operating Profit   588,200

Less Capital Expenses:

Property Taxes and License Fees	$ 81,000	
Depreciation	160,000	
Insurance	50,000	
Interest	230,000	521,000

Net Income Before Tax $ 67,200

$4,000 of the laundry expenses is fixed, $20,000 of the salaries and wages is fixed, $4,000 of the telephone service expense is fixed, $2,000 of the utilities expense is fixed, $1,000 of the advertising expense is fixed, all of the office supplies and dues are fixed, and all capital expenses are fixed. All other expenses are variable.

   a. Find the required percent occupancy per month to break even. (Assume a 30-day month.)

b.   Casa Rio has an offer from a national organization to
     hold a convention at the hotel if the firm will agree
     to give it 100 rooms at $40.00 per room per night for
     5 days. Casa Rio expects that if the convention were
     not held at the hotel, these rooms would be vacant.
     Should Casa Rio accept the offer? Why or why not?

c.   Suppose that the convention offer in part (b) is the
     same as before, but that the hotel expects it will
     have to turn away 30 customers per night who would
     have paid the $80 room rate. The convention offer is
     an all-or-nothing offer; therefore the hotel does not
     have the option of merely guaranteeing 70 rooms.
     Should Casa Rio accept the offer now? Why or why not?

Profit-Maximization Problems Involving Calculus (ref. EOCP C1-C9)

7. A farmer is trying to determine the profit-maximizing number of cattle that he should feed. He expects to receive a price of $540 for each steer (1 animal) that is brought to market. The total cost function is given by

$$TC = \$10{,}000 + 240Q - 10Q^2 + \tfrac{1}{3}Q^3, \text{ where } Q = \text{number}$$

of steers. How many steers should be fed and brought to market?

8. **(Use only if the appendix on mathematics of constrained optimization that follows Chapter 5 has been assigned.)**

Statue of Liberty Publishers, Inc., is getting ready to publish a non-fiction biography of a famous American that it hopes will be a great seller. SLP is also getting ready to publish a one-volume desk encyclopedia. At the present time, SLP must decide on the number of copies to be printed in the first press run for each book. The estimated demand function for the first 6 months for the encyclopedia is

$$Q_E = 5{,}600 - 100P_E,$$

where Q_E is quantity of encyclopedias and P_E is the price of one encyclopedia.

The corresponding demand function for the biography is

$$Q_B = 10{,}400 - 200P_B,$$

Where Q_B is the quantity of biographies and P_B is the price of one copy of the book.

The marginal cost of one copy of the encyclopedia is $6, and the marginal cost of one copy of the biography is $2. Assume that MC is constant for both books.

SLP is limited in printing press capacity over the relevant period to 3,500,000 pages. There are 400 pages in one copy of the encyclopedia and 500 pages in the biography.

a. Find the profit-maximizing values for Q_E, P_E, Q_B, and P_B.

b. Find the value of the Lagrangian multiplier. Interpret its meaning in this situation.

MULTIPLE CHOICE
Circle the letter that corresponds to the best answer.

1. Puttin' Purgatory is a miniature golf course located in Minneapolis. When winter comes, it is rational for the firm to eventually effect a temporary shut down because:
    (a) its fixed costs will rise dramatically;
    (b) golf balls get too hard when they are cold;
    (c) it is not likely to cover its variable costs;
    (d) the cross elasticity of demand between golf and football is negative.

2. Suppose a firm with a downward-sloping demand curve is operating where SMC < MR and P > AVC. It most definitely should:
    (a) cut its price and increase its output;
    (b) stay right where it is;
    (c) adjust output to the point where price equals its minimum AVC;
    (d) raise price.

3. A firm has $2,800 monthly fixed cost and charges a price of $40 per unit for its product. If AVC is 80 percent of its current price, what will be its break-even output?
    (a) 70 units per month;
    (b) 350 units per month;
    (c) 87.5 units per month;
    (d) impossible to determine from given data.

4. If a firm determines that (P - AVC) is greater than zero at the quantity where (MR - MC) = 0 but then becomes negative, it should;
    (a) raise price;
    (b) be at its profit maximum;
    (c) go to where P = MR;
    (d) temporarily shut down.

5. The difference between the change in revenue when output is increased and the change in cost for that same increase is called incremental or marginal:
    (a) revenue;
    (b) analysis;
    (c) profit;
    (d) revenue contribution.

Chapter 7.

HAND-IN PROBLEMS

Name_____

Course No. & Section_____

Problem 1.

SwissTime, a company that makes watches, has the revenue data given in the table below. Your instructor will supply the relevant cost data.

Q	P	TR	MR	MC	Mπ	TVC	AFC
0	$100					0	---
100	90						
200	80						
300	70						
400	60						
500	50						
600	40						

a. Complete the table.

b. What is the profit-maximizing price? _____

Quantity? _____ WHY?

Chapter 7.

HAND-IN PROBLEMS

Name_____

Course No. & Section_____

Problem 2.

Fernando Painting Company had the income statement given below for the month of September.

Income Statement
Fernando Painting Company
For the Month Ended September 30, 20XX

Total Sales (100,000 square ft. @ $____ per sq. ft. of $_____
            finished area)

Less Cost of Goods Sold:
    Direct Materials $_____
    Direct Labor   _____
    Variable "Manufacturing" Overhead   800
    Fixed "Manufacturing" Overhead   2,200   _____

Gross Profit   _____

Less Selling and Administrative Expenses:

    Gasoline Expense (Going to and $_____
        from jobs, getting
        materials)
    Variable Advertising Expense   300
    Fixed Selling and Administrative
        Expenses   800   _____

Net Income Before Taxes $_____

    a.   Find the monthly breakeven quantity (number of square foot units) for Fernando Painting.

b.   Fernando believes that if he lowers his price to
          $_____ per square foot of finished area he will
          increase quantity demanded to 125,000 square feet
          of finished wall per month. Should Fernando lower
          his price? Why or why not? (Assume *average*
          variable costs remain constant.)

Chapter 7.

HAND-IN PROBLEMS

Name_____

Course No. and Section_____

Problem 3.

Suppose a firm has the following total cost function for the short run:

$$STC = 4,000 + 60Q + 0.25Q^2,$$ so that its marginal

cost is MC = 60 + 0.50Q.

a. Determine its profit maximizing or loss minimizing output for the short run, given that the firm faces the following demand curve for its product:

$$Q = \underline{\hspace{2cm}} - 2P$$
    (Instructor supplied
       number)

so that its marginal revenue is

$$MR = \underline{\hspace{4cm}}$$
     (Instructor supplied equation)

b. What price should the firm charge for its product?

c. What will be the firm's short-run profit or loss?

Chapter 7.

HAND-IN PROBLEMS

Name_____

Course No. and Section_____

THIS PROBLEM REQUIRES CALCULUS

Problem 4.

Suppose that for a given time period a firm has the following demand curve:

$$Q = 205 - 0.25P$$

If its total cost function for the same period is:

$$STC = 800 + 500Q - 20Q^2 + \frac{1}{3}Q^3$$

find:

a. The sales quantity that will maximize its profit.

b. The price it should charge if profit is maximized.

c. The dollar value of its total profit at the maximum.

APPENDIX 7: Linear Programming and the Firm

PRACTICE PROBLEMS

Profit-Maximization Problems   (ref. Appendix problems 1-3)

1. As a result of a trucker's strike, Barker's Bakery is faced with limited amounts of powdered sugar, butter, and flour during the next week. Barker's has two products, sweet rolls and French bread. The profit contribution margin on a dozen sweet rolls is $1.20 and $.50 on a loaf of French bread. A dozen sweet rolls uses 1 lb. of powdered sugar, 2 lbs. of flour, and 1/4 lb. of butter. A loaf of French bread uses 2 lbs. of flour, no powdered sugar, and 1/8 lb. of butter. The bakery has available 60 lbs. of powdered sugar, 250 lbs. of flour, and 20 lbs. of butter. Use linear programming to indicate how many dozen rolls and loaves of bread Barker's should make.

>   (Use note paper to complete problem if space below is not
>   sufficient.)

2.   Set up the dual program for Barker's Bakery in Problem 1.
     a.   What is the optimal solution to this dual program?
     b   State the economic significance of the values of each
          of the dual variables at the optimal point.

3. Pat's Pots, Inc., produces two types of flower pots: plain red clay pots and painted pots. Pat's Pots has limited oven space, painter labor, and potter's wheels. In fact, the maximum number of oven hours available per day is 240 (12 hours X 20 pots capacity), the maximum painter labor hours is 24, and the maximum potter's wheel hours is 12. It takes 6 hours to bake both types of pots, .2 hour on the potter's wheel for a plain red pot and .4 hour for a painted pot, and 1 hour of painter labor for a painted pot. The profit contribution of a plain red pot is $4 while that of a painted pot is $6. Using linear programming, find the optimal quantities of red and painted pots that Pat's Pots should produce each day.

(Use note paper to complete problem if space below is not sufficient.)

4. Set up the dual program for Pat's Pots in Problem 3.
    a. What economic interpretation can be given to each of
        the dual decision variables, the objective function,
        and the constraints?

    b. What is the optimal solution to the dual program?

Cost Minimization Problem (ref. Appendix problem 4)

5.   Shoes R We is trying to determine the optimal mix of store types to use to sell its shoes.   The two types of stores under consideration are stores inside large suburban shopping malls and "stand alone" stores in central city areas.   It will cost $20,000 a month to lease space for a store in a large mall but only $15,000 to lease space in the central city.

Although the cost factor is certainly a consideration, each type of store does have advantages.   The average number of people walking past a typical mall store is 6,000 a day, whereas the average daily number walking past a downtown store is 8,000. However, SRW estimates that there are an average of 800 families with annual incomes over $20,000 that live within 2 miles of the typical mall store, while there are only 400 families with incomes over $20,000 that live the same distance from a downtown store. SRW believes that either type of store will have an average of 4,000 households that have a TV set (so that they can see television ads) within a four-mile radius of each store.   SRW wishes to have its stores located so that an average of at least 120,000 people walk past its stores each day, there are an average of at least 9,600 families with annual incomes over $20,000 that live within 2 miles of the stores, and that an average of at least 72,000 households with a TV set will live within four miles of its stores.

   a. Given the information above, how many of each type of store should the firm lease if it wishes to minimize leasing costs?
       (Use note paper to complete problem if space below is not sufficient.)

b. What is the total cost to the firm of leasing these
    stores at its optimal point?

c. What is the marginal cost to the firm of increasing
    the income constraint? The television constraint?

Appendix 7.

HAND-IN PROBLEMS

Name_____

Course No. and Section_____

Problem 1.

Santex Specialties, Inc. produces two articles made of cloth, men's shirts and pillowcases. The firm has access to three inputs that are owned by another company and available in limited amounts-- the cutting machine, the sewing machine, and the buttonhole machine. Production of one gross of men's shirts requires 2 hours of cutting machine time, one hour of sewing machine time, and 2 hours of buttonhole machine time. A gross of pillowcases can be produced with 1.5 hours of cutting machine time, 0.5 hours of sewing machine time, and no use of the buttonhole machine. Given its arrangement with the company that owns the machinery, the maximum amounts of machine time per week that Santex can obtain are: 12 hours cutting machine; 5 hours sewing machine; and 8 hours buttonhole machine.

a. In the space below, sketch the feasible space for Santex's production of the two goods. (Put shirts on the vertical axis of your diagram.)

b. If a gross of shirts yields a profit contribution of _____,
                              (instructor supplied number)

   while a gross of pillowcases has a _____ profit contribu-
                              (instructor supplied number)
   tion, what will be the algebraic setup of this linear programming problem, using the concept of slack variables?

(continued next page)

c. Show the algebra for the optimum solution, and indicate the maximum weekly profit contribution possible. (You may find the appropriate corner graphically and show the solution for just this one corner.)

Appendix 7.

HAND-IN PROBLEMS

Name_____

Course No. and Section_____

Problem 2.

Metro Metals Co. (a subsidiary of Channel 1 News) makes only two products, claw hammers and a small revolver known as the Travis Special. The production process requires only three types of equipment: forging equipment, lathes, and welding equipment. With its present factory, Metro Metals has available on a daily basis 120 machine-hours of forging capacity, 50 machine-hours of welding capacity, and 80 machine-hours of lathe capacity. It estimates the per unit profit contribution of claw hammers to be

_____each and that of revolvers to be _____ each.
(instructor supplied number)   (instructor supplied number)

The production of one revolver requires 0.2 machine-hours of forging, 0.2 machine-hours of welding, and 0.4 machine-hours of lathe work. It takes 0.3 machine-hours of forging, 0.1 machine-hours of welding, and no lathe work to produce one claw hammer.

a. In the space below, write the total profit contribution function for Metro Metals, and set up the system of equations (or inequalities) necessary to maximize that function using linear programming.

(continued next page)

b. Next graph the feasible space for Metro Metals. Put hammers
   on the vertical axis of your diagram.

c. Use the graphical method to identify the linear programming
   solution to Metro's problem, and show the algebra for the
   solution below. Provide answers for the quantities produced
   and for the firm's total profit contribution.

d. Set up the dual program for Metro Metals, but do not solve it.
        (Attach additional sheet if needed.)

CHAPTER 8: Perfect Competition and Monopoly

Programmed Review

This chapter deals primarily with application of the profit maximizing approach of Chapter 5 to the two limiting cases in the broad spectrum of possible product market structures that a firm can face. Fundamentally, market structure in the firm's product market refers to the nature of the _____ curve the firm faces as well as the number of buyers and sellers in the market and how they react to one another.

demand

At one end of the spectrum is perfect competition, a market structure characterized by a _____ number of buyers and sellers of a product that is _____ or identical from seller to seller, no government controls or interference, _____ knowledge of market conditions, and _____ entry or exit of firms in the long run. In a perfectly competitive market, independently acting buyers and sellers eventually generate an _____ price at which quantity demanded equals quantity _____. The individual firm is powerless to affect this price and must take it as given. Thus, the market price becomes the _____ curve of the firm. In the usual demand curve quadrant, this demand curve turns out to be a _____ line, representing not only the market price but also the marginal _____ of the firm.

large

homogeneous

perfect

free

equilibrium

supplied

demand

horizontal

revenue

The perfectly competitive firm, whether in the short run or the long, maximizes profit where market price equals _____ cost, assuming the latter is rising. Thus, quantity produced and sold is determined by the firm, but not the

marginal

price. At the firm's best output (where MC = MR) it will decide to produce, rather than shut down, in the short run as long as price is greater than its _____ _____ cost. If price   <u>average variable</u> is greater than the firm's short-run average cost (SAC), profit will be _____ than normal.   <u>greater</u> If price is less than SAC but greater than average variable cost, a loss minimum will occur where _____ _____ is equal to price. In the long   <u>marginal</u> <u>cost</u> run, a perfectly competitive will tend to have _____ profit, since free entry and exit will   <u>normal</u> cause above or below normal profits to be eliminated.

In pure monopoly, there is only one _____   <u>seller</u> of a given good or service. The firm's demand curve in this case is the same as the _____   <u>market</u> demand curve. Thus, marginal revenue will be _____ than price. A monopolist maximizes profit   <u>less</u> where marginal revenue equals _____ cost and   <u>marginal</u> must set the price that is consistent with sales of the profit-maximizing _____. If the   <u>quantity</u> correct price is not set, profit will not be maximized.

In the short run, a monopoly firm may have greater than normal profit, but its other possibilities include normal profit, operation at a loss-minimizing level of output, or temporary shut down. The latter is rational if _____ is   <u>price</u> less than average variable cost at the output where marginal cost equals _____ _____.   <u>marginal</u> <u>revenue</u> In the long run, a monopoly may have either normal profit or greater than normal profit. There is no tendency for greater than normal profits to be eliminated, since _____ by new firms is not   <u>entry</u> possible. The monopoly model is very important

in managerial economics, since other types of
firms that face downward-sloping demand curves
are analytically similar to the monopoly case.

PRACTICE PROBLEMS

Diagrams of Perfect Competition and Monopoly   (ref. EOCP 1)

1. Complete the following diagram to show a perfectly competitive firm minimizing loss where MC = MR in the short run.

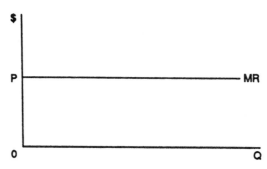

2. Complete the following diagram to show a monopoly with normal profit in the long run.

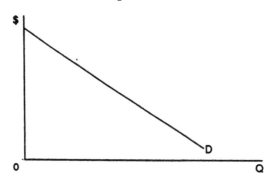

3. Complete the following diagram to show a perfectly competitive firm with only normal profit in the short run.

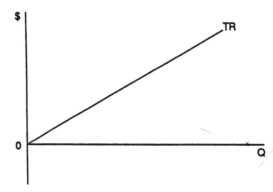

Getting Started:
   Be careful not to mix total curves with marginal and average curves. It is a good idea to locate the profit-maximizing quantity first.

Tabular Problems on Competition and Monopoly.
       (ref. EOCP 2, 6, 7, 8)

   4. Complete the following table, where Q is quantity sold
       and revenue and cost data are in dollars.

	P	Q	TR	STC	AVC	TVC	
MR	20		600		20.00	600	MC
	20	40		770			
		50	1000	800			3
	20	60		840			
	20		1400	900	10.71	750	
		80	1600	1050			
	20	90			14.33	1290	

   a) What type of market structure is indicated by the
      data in the table, assuming no contractual or
      regulatory constraints on the firm's price? Explain.

   b) Employ the marginal condition for profit maximization
      to determine which of the above quantities sold will
      yield the greatest profit. What is the amount of
      this profit?

   c) Could the above short-run equilibrium also be a long-run
      one for the firm? Why or why not?

<u>Getting Started</u>:
The definitions of the various revenue and cost concepts are the key to filling in the table. The firm is willing to increase Q if there is, or eventually is, a range where increasing Q adds more to revenue than to cost. Approach the problem below in the same way.

5. Complete the table below, where Q is quantity sold and all revenue and cost data are in dollars.

P	Q	TR	MR	TC	MC
10	20	200		100	
	40				6
8	60		6	300	
7	80	560			7
	100		2		11
	120		0	980	

a) The firm above represents a monopoly situation and cannot be representative of perfect competition. Explain why.

b) Identify the price and output combination in the table that yields the greatest profit. What marginal condition must occur in the neighborhood of this maximum?

c) What is the value of profit at its maximum? Does the firm have to charge the price above in order to obtain the maximum profit? Why?

Profit Maximization Using Equations. (ref. EOCP 3, 4, and 9)

6. Suppose a monopoly firm faces the following market demand curve:

$$Q = 960 - 20P, \text{ so that its marginal}$$

revenue is MR = 48 - 0.1Q.

If its short-run total cost function is:

$$TC = 3,000 + 4Q + 0.06Q^2, \text{ so that its}$$

marginal cost is MC = 4 + 0.12Q

a) What will be its profit-maximizing quantity and price?
   (Show calculations.)

$$44 - 0.22Q = 0$$
$$44 = .22Q$$

$$20p = 960 - Q$$
$$p = 48 - \tfrac{1}{20}Q$$
$$P(Q)Q = 48Q - \tfrac{1}{20}Q^2 = TR$$
$$200 = Q$$
$$38 = P$$
$$48 - .10Q - 4 - 0.12Q = 44$$

b) How much profit will the firm have at the above price and quantity?

$$TR - TC = TP$$
$$TR = 200(38) = 7,600$$
$$TC = 3000 + 4(200) + 0.06(200)^2 = 6,200$$
$$= \$1,400$$

<u>Getting Started</u>:
   Solve by applying the marginal condition for maximizing profit. Do the same on the problem below.

7. A perfectly competitive firm faces a market price of $40 and has the following total and marginal cost functions:

$$STC = 5800 + 20Q + 0.02Q^2$$

$$SMC = 20 + 0.04Q$$

a) What quantity of output is best for this firm in the short run. Why?
   (Show calculations.)

b) Should the firm attempt to charge some price other than the market price of $40? Why or why not?

THE FOLLOWING PROBLEMS REQUIRE CALCULUS (ref. EOCP C1-C8)

8. Suppose a monopoly firm has the following total cost function for the short run:

$$STC = 700 + 90Q - 10Q^2 + \frac{1}{3}Q^3$$

a) Determine its profit maximizing or loss minimizing output for the short run, given that the firm faces the following demand curve for its product:

$$Q = 58 - 0.2P$$

b) What price should the firm charge for its product?

c) What will be the firm's short-run profit or loss?

<u>Getting Started</u>:
Use the calculus to get marginal revenue and marginal cost. Then proceed as in problems 2 and 3. Do the same below.

9. Napier Corporation has estimated its short-run total cost function to be the following:

$$STC = 10,500 + 290Q - 2Q^2 + .01Q^3, \text{ where \$10,500 is}$$
its total fixed cost.

It has also estimated a long-run total cost function and has come up with the following:

$$LTC = 425Q - 1.5Q^2 + .002Q^3.$$

Answer the questions below.

a) What is Napier's short-run <u>average</u> cost at an output of Q = 100?

b) If Napier operates in a perfectly competitive market and faces a market price of $190, what will be its short-run output level and profit (or loss)?

c) Suppose Napier operates in a perfectly competitive industry.   When   the   <u>industry</u>   is   in   long-run equilibrium, what will be Napier's quantity produced, price, and profit.
   (Show necessary calculations.)

MULTIPLE CHOICE
    Circle the letter that corresponds to the best answer.

1. The short-run supply curve of the individual perfectly
    competitive firm:
    -(a) is its marginal cost where above AVC;
    (b) is completely inelastic;
    (c) cannot be logically determined;
    (d) is horizontal.

2. One thing monopoly has in common with perfect competition is:
    (a) The demand curve of the firm is downward sloping;
    (b) The firm never operates at a loss;
    (c) The firm must take rivals' behavior into account and
         plan accordingly;
    -(d) Profit is maximized where MC = MR.

3. Suppose a monopoly faces a downward-sloping demand curve and
    is operating where MR < 0. It should:
    -(a) raise price;
    (b) set price equal to quantity;
    (c) go to minimum short-run average cost;
    (d) none of the above.

4. Suppose a firm is operating where MC = MR in the short run
    and that its AFC at that point is $2 per unit. Suppose also
    that its TVC at that point is $600. If its profit-maximizing
    output per week is 100 units which are sold at a price of
    $10 each, what will be its weekly total profit?
    -(a) $200;
    (b) $2,000;
    (c) zero or normal profit;
    (d) Profit cannot be determined from the given information.

5. A monopoly that is attempting to minimize its short-run loss,
    should:
    (a) maximize total revenue;
    (b) make sure price is greater than AFC;
    -(c) operate where SAC is minimum;
    D   (d) either operate where MC = MR or shut down.

Chapter 8.

HAND-IN PROBLEMS

Name_____ ,

Course No. and Section_____

Problem 1.

Pluto Corporation operates under highly competitive market conditions where management believes it must charge the going

market price of $_____ for its output. The Company has the
              **(Instructor supplied
                   number.)**

following total and marginal cost functions:

$$STC = 20,000 + 200Q - 10Q^2 + \frac{1}{3}Q^3$$

$$SMC = 200 - 20Q + Q^2$$

a) What is Pluto's marginal revenue? Why?

b)   What quantity of output is best for Pluto in the short run. Why? (Show calculations.)

c) How much profit, if any, will Pluto have at the best output?

Chapter 8.

HAND-IN PROBLEMS

Name_____

Course No. and Section_____

Problem 2.

Graph the three following cases.

<---1. _____

_____

_____

_____
(Instructor supplied
case)

2. _____ --->

_____

_____

_____
(Instructor supplied
case)

<---3. _____

_____

_____

_____
(Instructor supplied
case)

Chapter 8.

HAND-IN PROBLEMS

Name_____

Course No. and Section_____

Problem 3.

Suppose a monopoly firm has estimated the following demand curve:

$$Q = \underline{\hspace{1cm}} - 2P, \text{ so that MR } = \underline{\hspace{1cm}} - Q.$$
(Instructor supplied numbers)

a) What combination of price and quantity will yield the maximum <u>total revenue</u> for the firm?

b) Now suppose that total and marginal cost for this firm are described by the following equations:

$$STC = 4,000 + 30Q + 0.25Q^2$$

$$SMC = 30 + 0.5Q$$

Determine its profit maximizing or loss minimizing output for the short run.

c) What price should the firm charge for its product, and what will be its profit at the maximum?

Chapter 8.

HAND-IN PROBLEMS

Name_____

Course No. and Section_____

THIS PROBLEM REQUIRES CALCULUS

Problem 4.

Joisey Corporation has estimated its short-run total cost function to be the following:

$$STC = 8,000 + 200Q - 2Q^2 + .01Q^3, \text{ where \$8,000 is its total fixed cost.}$$

It has also estimated a long-run total cost function and has come up with the following:

$$LTC = 340Q - 2.4Q^2 + .008Q^3.$$

Answer the questions below.

a) Given Joisey's estimate of its LTC function, is its plant size appropriate for an output of Q = 100? Explain.

b) What is the minimum short-run average variable cost (AVC) Joisey can attain in its current plant?

c) Suppose Joisey operates in a perfectly competitive industry. When the industry is in long-run equilibrium, what will be Joisey's quantity produced, price, and profit. (Show necessary calculations; attach additional sheet if needed.)

CHAPTER 9: Monopolistic Competition and Oligopoly

Programmed Review

This chapter is about the many real-world markets that lie between the two extremes of perfect competition and monopoly. It begins with a discussion of monopolistic competition, a market structure that has a large number of buyers and sellers but is characterized by products that are slightly _____ as compared to the homogeneous product found in perfect competition.

       differentiated

The monopolistically competitive firm believes it faces a demand curve that is _____ elastic but not perfectly elastic. Based on this estimate of demand, to maximize profit the firm sets a _____ consistent with equating marginal revenue with _____ _____.   The firm may try to increase its market share through _____ _____. In the long run, its profit will be normal, since there is free _____.

       highly

       price
       marginal cost
       product
       differentiation
       entry

The general term for a market with few sellers is _____. In this type of market, each seller pays a great deal of attention to the strategy of the other firms, since firms view each other as _____. A two-firm oligopoly is called a _____. Under the assumptions made by Cournot, a costless duopoly will supply two-thirds of the quantity that would be demanded at a price of _____. Even with only two firms, a variety of results is possible depending on how one firm _____ to a decision made by the other.

       oligopoly

       rivals
       duopoly

       zero

       reacts

An oligopolistic market in which rivals will follow a price cut but not a price increase is described by the _____ demand curve model. The marginal revenue curve for such a demand curve

       kinked

has a _____ in it. This feature helps to explain   gap

why the firm might not alter its price, even if

there is a change in its _____ cost.   marginal

     In the dominant firm model of price leader-

ship, there is one _____ firm, and there are   large

many _____ ones that follow the price lead of   small

the former. The demand curve of the dominant firm

is obtained by subtracting the supply curve of

the small firms from the _____ _____   market demand

curve.

The equilibrium price is determined by the large

firm and is consistent with the quantity sold

that equates the firm's marginal revenue with

its _____ _____.   marginal cost

     If oligopolistic firms perfectly collude,

they will form a _____. The allocation of   cartel

output that results in maximizing the cartel's

profit requires that the _____ cost of pro-   marginal

duction be the same in each firm and equal also

to _____ _____ from sales. This rule   marginal revenue

for allocation of output can apply to a multiple

plant firm as well as a cartel. The cases dis-

cussed in this chapter are but a few in the broad

range of oligopolistic market situations that

can occur. Since most real-world firms fall into

the catch-all category of oligopoly, many of the

tools applied in this chapter can be used to ana-

lyze them on a case-by-case basis.

PRACTICE PROBLEMS

Problem on Monopolistic Competition   (ref. EOCP 1,2)

1.   Briefly explain what is wrong with the following diagram of
     a monopolistically competitive firm.   Explain how the firm
     would have to adjust in order to reach a short-run profit max-
     imizing position.

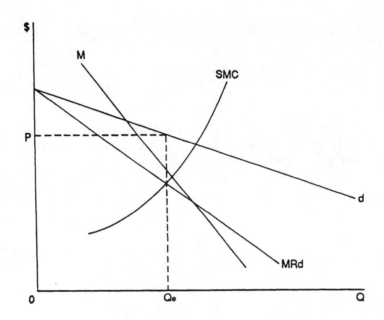

Getting Started:
     Ask yourself how the M curve must be re
     lated to the firm's profit-maximizing quan-
     tity and price, as well as to the quantity
     where its MC equals its MR.

The Duopoly Case   (ref. EOCP 3)

2.   Your university has authorized two student clubs to collect
     parking fees at the practice field on the days of every
     home football game.   The university allows the clubs to keep
     all receipts, and labor is furnished free by the club memb-
     ers.   You are a member of one of the two clubs.

     You have estimated that the per game demand for parking at
     the field is described by the following equation:

$$Q = 3200 - 400P$$

a. What strategy will maximize the revenues of the two
    clubs, and what price is consistent with this stra-
    tegy?

b. If the two clubs proceed as duopolists under the
    conditions described by Cournot, what price will each
    charge? Explain.

c. Compare the revenues under the Cournot assumption with
    those that would be obtained if the clubs acted like
    a single monopolist.

Getting Started:
        Maximizing the joint revenues (acting like
        a monopolist) will yield more revenue than
        Cournot's solution. Since the demand curve
        is linear, ask where the MR = 0. The Cour-
        not solution tells what will happen if
        each seller believes the other will keep
        quantity constant.

Price Leadership by a Dominant Firm (ref. EOCP 4, 5)

3. Kersplash Corp. is the nation's largest producer of toilet flush valves. Kersplash typically charges a standard price for a flush valve that fits many different brands of toilets. Kersplash's management realizes that its industry is characterized by a relatively large number of smaller firms that are followers in the sense that they will always charge exactly the price that Kersplash sets.

   Currently, Kersplash estimates that the market demand curve for the valves has the following equation:

   $$Q_d = 8,520 - 110P .$$

   Kersplash knows that its own total costs can be represented by the equation

   $$TC_L = 100,000 + 3.2Q + .001Q^2.$$

   so that $MC_L = 3.2 + .002Q$ is its marginal cost.

   In addition, it has estimated that the smaller firms' supply curve can be represented by the equation $Q_s = 20 + 15P.$

   a. Write the equation for the demand curve facing Kersplash.

   $$Q_L = Q_d - Q_s = (8,520 - 110P) - (20 + 15P)$$
   $$Q_L = 8,500 - 125P$$

   b. It can be determined from the above demand curve that marginal revenue for Kersplash will be $MR_L = 68 - .016Q_L$. Determine the price that Kersplash will charge and the quantity of output that it will sell.

   $$68 - .016 Q_L = 3.2 + .002 Q_L$$
   $$Q_L = 3,600$$

c. Determine the quantity that the smaller firms will
   supply and the market quantity demanded.

d. What is the total profit of Kersplash Corp.?

   Getting Started:
   This problem and the next both require
   that you first define the demand curve of
   the dominant firm. Thereafter, proceed
   as in an ordinary profit maximizing
   problem.

THE FOLLOWING PROBLEM REQUIRES CALCULUS   (ref. EOCP C5)

4. Suppose the widget industry consists of a large, domin-
    ant firm and a great number of small firms. The   total
    cost function of the large firm is

$$TC_L = 1,000 + 5Q + 0.75Q^2$$

If the supply function of the small firms is described
by the equation $Q_s = 500 + 3P$ and market demand for wid-
gets is $Q_d = 5,000 - P$, assuming the small firms will
follow the price lead of the large one, determine:

    a. the price that the large firm will establish
    b. the quantity supplied by the large firm;
    c. the quantity supplied by the small firms;
    d. the quantity that consumers will purchase.

Kinked Demand Curve Oligopoly.   (ref. EOCP 9)

5. Canauba Carpet Co. operates in a large metropolitan area
    where the market for carpet sold to home builders is char-
    acterized by a great deal of interfirm rivalry. When
    one firm cuts price, others seem always to follow suit.

However, if a firm raises price, it is unlikely that others will too.

Suppose Canauba estimates that, given its current price and quantity of carpet sold per week, its demand curve is represented by the equation $Q_1 = 2,100 - 100P$ for price cuts but by the equation $Q_2 = 3,300 - 200P$ for price increases. (In either equation, the Q term is the number of square yards of carpet sold per week to home builders.)

a. What is Canauba Carpet Co.'s current price? How many square yards of carpet is it selling to home builders per week?

b. The two stated demand functions yield the following equations for marginal revenue:

$$MR_1 = 21 - .02Q_1$$

$$MR_2 = 16.5 - .01Q_2$$

If Canauba's total cost function for supplying carpet to the builders is

$$TC = 2400 + 0.75Q + 0.005Q^2$$

so that its marginal cost is $MC = 0.75 + 0.01Q$

is the current price it charges in (a) consistent with profit maximization? Explain.

c. What range of marginal cost values at the quantity calculated in (a) would lead the firm to charge the price in (a)? Explain.

Getting Started:
In this problem as well as the one below, start by finding out where the two demand curves intersect. Then find the gap in MR and determine whether or not the firm's MC curve passes through it.

THE FOLLOWING PROBLEM REQUIRES CALCULUS   (ref. EOCP C2, C4, C6.)

6. Noodle Corporation of America (NCA) operates in a
    non-collusive oligopolistic market where firms tend to
    base their strategies on good old fashioned fear. NCA be-
    lieves that at its current price its demand curve will
    be Q = 440 - 4P if it raises price, since it expects that
    other firms will not follow a price increase. However,
    for price cuts it believes its demand curve is
    Q = 250 - 2P, since other firms are expected to follow a
    reduction in price.

    a. With the above assumptions, what are NCA's current
       price and quantity sold?

    b. Suppose NCA's total cost function is:

       $$STC = 50 + 20Q - 0.1Q^2 + 0.004Q^3$$

       Is NCA maximizing its profit at the quantity and price
       you found in (1)? Explain why or why not.

    c. Now suppose that NCA has made an error in its esti-
       mate of the total cost function so that the actual
       total cost is:

       $$STC = 60 + 20Q - 0.1Q^2 + 0.006Q^3$$

       With this revised total cost function, what is the
       firm's profit-maximizing price and output?

Operation of a Multiple-Plant Firm (same as cartel model)
(ref. EOCP 7)

7. The government of Western Pacifica has a salt-marketing monopoly. However, it buys all of its salt from local producers who are guaranteed a price of $150 per ton. You and your pal, Bwana Jim, have three salt mines with the following marginal costs of production:

$$MC_a = 10 + .008Q_a$$

$$MC_b = 40 + .002Q_b$$

$$MC_c = 6 + .015Q_c,$$ where the Q term refers to the monthly output of each mine.

What allocation of production to the three mines is consistent with profit maximization? If you and Jim have monthly fixed costs of $2 million, and the respective average variable costs of production in the mines at the optimum allocation are $AVC_a = \$80$, $AVC_b = \$95$, and $AVC_c = 78$, what will your total profit be?

<u>Getting Started</u>:
Use the rule for allocating output to cartel members to solve for each mine's output quantity. Then calculate the gross TR and the TC, keeping in mind that each mine has different variable costs.

MULTIPLE CHOICE
Circle the letter that corresponds to the best answer.

1. A firm that is in monopolistic competition (not monopoly)
    differs from one in perfect competition because:
    (a) it faces a downsloping demand curve;
    (b) it always has increasing returns to scale;
    (c) entry into its market is severely limited;
    (d) it has no concept of marginal cost.

2. Suppose an oligopolistic firm is operating where MR = MC,
    price is greater than AVC, marginal profit is zero and
    falling, but fixed costs are not covered. It should:
    (a) cut price to sell more;
    (b) raise price;
    (c) temporarily shut down;
    (d) make no change in its price or quantity produced.

    $P > AVC$
    $MP = 0 \downarrow$

3. Suppose a firm is operating in an oligopoly market and faces
    a kinked demand curve. For price <u>increases</u> the equation of
    the demand curve is Q = 1800 - 10P, while for price <u>decreases</u>
    it is Q = 1000 - 5P. Assuming the firm's MC curve passes
    through the gap in its MR curve, which of the following will
    be its equilibrium price:
    (a) $160;
    (b) $140;
    (c) $100;
    (d) none of the above.

    $1800 - 10p = 1000 - 5p$
    $-5p = -800$
    $P = 160$

4. In a monopolistically competitive industry (not monopoly)
    greater than normal profits are eliminated in the long run
    by:
    (a) government regulation;
    (b) price wars among firms;
    (c) a horizontal demand curve;
    (d) none of the above.

5. One thing oligopoly has in common with perfect competition
    is:
    (a) no one firm has any market power;
    (b) all firms tend to charge the same price;
    (c) firms must take rivals' behavior into account and plan
        accordingly;
    (d) profit is maximized where MC = MR.

Chapter 9.

HAND-IN PROBLEMS

Name_____

Course No. and Section_____

Problem 1.

Basic Corporation of America (BCA) operates in an oligopolistic market. Although firms in this market do not collude, each one fears that the others will always try to offset its pricing policy in the worst way--that is, by following a price cut but failing to follow a price increase. BCA believes that at its current price its demand curve will be $Q_1 = 220 - P$ if it cuts price, since it expects that other firms will follow a price decrease. However, for price increases it believes its

demand curve is _____, since other firms are <u>not</u>
                (instructor supplied equation)
expected to follow an increase in price.

   a. With the above assumptions, what are BCA's current price and quantity sold?

   b. The Q_1 demand curve yields $MR_1 = 220 - 2Q_1$, while that for Q_2 yields $MR_2 = 180 - Q_2$. Suppose BCA's marginal cost function is:

$$MC_1 = 30 - 0.2Q + 0.012Q^2$$

   Is BCA maximizing its profit at the quantity and price you found in (1)? Explain why or why not.

(continued next page)

(Ch. 9 Problem 1, continued)

c. Now suppose that BCA has made an error in its estimate
   of the marginal cost function so that the actual marginal
   cost is:

$$MC_2 = 90 + 0.25Q$$

With this revised marginal cost function, what is the
firm's profit-maximizing price and output?

Chapter 9.

HAND-IN PROBLEMS

Name_____

Course No. and Section_____

Problem 2.

Qwerty corporation has two plants that produce its single product. The equation of the demand curve it faces is

Q = _____.   The table on the left below shows the behavior
    (instructor supplied equation)
of marginal cost, MC_1 and MC_2, in the two plants, where Q_1 is the output in Plant 1 and Q_2 is the output in Plant 2.

Q_1	MC_1	Q_2	MC_2	Q Sold	Price	TR	MR
0		0		0			
2	3.0	2	2.5	2			
4	5.0	4	5.5	4			
6	9.5	6	9.0	6			
8	11.0	8	10.2	8			
10	14.8	10	13.0	10			
12	17.2	12	15.5	12			
14	22.0	14	18.5	14			
16	26.5	16	22.0	16			

a. Use the given demand curve equation to fill in the price and revenue data in the table on the right above.

b. Determine the amount of production in each plant that is consistent with profit maximization for Qwerty. Explain how you determined these amounts.

c. If the relevant total fixed costs for the above data are $40 for Plant 1 and $32 for Plant 2, how much will the firm's total profit be?

Chapter 9.

HAND-IN PROBLEMS

Name_____

Course No. and Section_____

Problem 3.   (REQUIRES CALCULUS)

Sparkola Corp. is the nation's largest producer of rebuilt automobile starters to fit cars built by General Motors. Sparkola typically charges a standard price for any starter to fit a GM auto. Sparkola's management realizes that its industry is characterized by a relatively large number of smaller firms that are followers in the sense that they will always charge exactly the price that Sparkola sets.

Currently, Sparkola estimates that the market demand curve for the starters has the following equation:

$$Q_d = 7,760 - 75P .$$

Sparkola knows that its own marginal costs of production can be represented by the equation $MC = 1.25 + .005Q$. In addition, it has estimated that the smaller firms' supply curve can be represented by the equation $Q_s = 10 + 25P$.

a. Write the equation for the demand curve facing Sparkola.

b. Determine the price that Sparkola will charge and the quantity of output that it will sell.

c. Determine the quantity that the smaller firms will supply and the market quantity demanded.

CHAPTER 10: Games, Information, and Strategy

Programmed Review

This chapter focuses mainly on situations where firms view each other as rivals, and each one must consider the other's actions when developing a strategy. A strategy is a _____ or a sequence thereof made by a decision maker. In the first part of the chapter, a theoretical approach to strategic behavior was discussed. This approach, known as _____ theory has numerous dimensions. For example, there is the single-period, simultaneous-move game, also called a ____-_____ game. The text presented a number of two-player examples of this type of game, where possible outcomes were analyzed using a _____ matrix.

<u>choice</u>

<u>game</u>

<u>one</u> - <u>shot</u>

<u>payoff</u>

It is most important in analyzing a game to ascertain whether or not a player will chose a specific course of action no matter what the other player(s) choose to do; that is, to determine whether or not the player has a _____ strategy. When each player is doing the best that he or she can, *given* the other's strategy, there is a _____ equilibrium in the game. Using a two-player discount game, the chapter showed that such an equilibrium can occur when both or just one of the players has a dominant strategy. A player can decide what to do by examining the possible outcomes and identifying the _____ strategies of a rival. This approach is known as an _____ dominance strategy.

<u>dominant</u>

<u>Nash</u>

<u>dominated</u>

<u>iterative</u>

Sometimes a game will have multiple Nash equilibria. Then it may not be possible to determine the outcome. The outcome, however, may be

determinable if the game is not a simultaneous
one, in other words, if it is a _____ game.   <u>sequential</u>
Then, one player, having seen what the other has
done, may clearly be best off to make a choice
consistent with just one of the Nash equilibria.
An interesting feature of sequential games has
to do with a benefit that accrues to the player
making the first strategic choice. This player
may have a _____-_____ advantage, which en-   <u>first</u> - <u>mover</u>
sures he/she will be better off than otherwise
possible, given the reactions available to the
other player. A _____ diagram can be used to   <u>tree</u>
analyze a sequential game.

Another important consideration in game theory
has to do with situations where one player may
impose some sort of punishment on another. This
type of game involves a threat. The outcome is
likely to depend on whether the threat is per-
ceived as a _____ one.   <u>credible</u>

Information is also important in the devel-
opment of a firm's _____. Generally, in-   <u>strategy</u>
formation is not free. Both firms and consumers
incur costs, called _____ costs, to obtain   <u>search</u>
information that aids in decision making. In a
transaction, a party on one side may have better
information than the other party to the agreement.
This is a case of _____ information.   <u>asymmetric</u>
Certain cases of asymmetric information yield
unfavorable results because of adverse selection,
which is exemplified by the *lemons* problem in
the used car market. There, it is argued that
buyers, who generally have imperfect information,
view all cars as possible lemons and, therefore,
offer only low prices for them. Sellers of good
cars opt out of the market, since they do not

want to accept the low price, leaving only
_____ in the market.   <u>lemons</u>

    Imperfect information and adverse selection
also occur in insurance markets, and they are
compounded by risky behavior of insured parties,
reflecting a phenomenon called _____ hazard.   <u>moral</u>
There is moral hazard when a party who is insured
against loss behaves in a way that increases the
risk of it. Principal-agent relationships in
business can also be complicated by moral hazard, especially when one party to a transaction
has information unobservable to another, known
as _____ information. Problems involving   <u>private</u>
such information can often be mitigated by
monitoring or by a process which reveals what
otherwise would be kept secret. In addition,
where rewards are related to a desired behavioral
outcome, contracts that promote the behavior,
known as _____ contracts, can be employed   <u>incentive</u>
to protect the party with imperfect information.
Finally, there are cases where a party may wish
to communicate to another that he or she will
not engage in undesirable behaviors. For example,
a college graduate may come to a job interview
dressed very nicely and carrying a laptop compu-
ter, thereby giving the interviewer a _____   <u>signal</u>
that she is seriously ready to get down to work.

PRACTICE PROBLEMS

Game Theory
   (ref. EOCP 1, 2, 3)

1.   Two pizza chains, Mamma Mia's and Pizza Palace, are considering the strategy of accepting or not accepting competitors' coupons. Below are the profit payoffs, in millions of dollars per year, from the two alternative strategies. (Data pertaining to Mamma Mia's in boldface type.) Assume that each firm does not know what the other's strategy will be but does know what the outcome will be *if* a given choice is made by its rival. This is a one-shot game.

PIZZA PALACE

	Don't Accept Coupons		Accept Coupons	
Don't Accept Coupons	**40**	60	**35**	90
MAMMA MIA'S				
Accept Coupons	**30**	70	**45**	80

a.   Does Mamma Mia's have a dominant strategy? Explain.

b.   Does Pizza Palace have a dominant strategy? Explain.

c.   Determine the outcome of the game, and explain why it will occur.

2.   Two rival air carriers, Allied Airlines (AA) and Unbeatable
      Airways (UA), are considering special offers during mid-
      February for Valentine's travel. Each must decide whether
      to offer a low-priced ticket ($280 plus taxes and fees) to
      London or Paris or offer double frequent-flyer miles on any
      type of ticket. Below are their expected payoff outcomes in
      terms of additional passenger revenues in millions of dollars.

                                       UA

                          Fare Special   Double Miles

		Fare Special		Double Miles	
AA	**Fare Special**	2.5 *A*	2.0 *V*	3.0 *A*	1.8
	Double Miles	2.0	1.8	2.7	2.1 *U*

a.   Does either firm have a dominant strategy? Explain.

                          AA

b.   Discuss the outcome of this game.

3.   Two rival supermarket chains, Safeger's and Ralphson's are
      the major players in retail groceries in a western state.
      Currently, both offer "shoppers' club" cards that provide
      discounts to members. Industry profits are sagging, and both
      firms are looking into eliminating the card program. The
      matrix that follows shows the payoffs (impact on quarterly
      profit in million dollars) from either keeping or eliminating
      the cards.

Safeger's

Keep Cards — Eliminate Cards

	Keep Cards	Eliminate Cards
Keep Cards	**130** 105	**112** 90
Eliminate Cards	90 110	**120** 130

Ralphson's

a.   Does either firm have a dominant strategy? Explain why or why not.

b.   If this is a one-shot, simultaneous game, what can we say about the outcome?

c.   If the game is sequential and Ralphson's moves first, can we predict the outcome? Explain.

d.   Is there a first-mover advantage in this game? If so, identify it. If not, suggest a change in the data that would create such an advantage, and explain why it occurs.

4.   A domestic air carrier, Trans Nation (TN) is considering a change in service that will replace ageing narrow-body short-haul jets with new, wide-body aircraft. Since the firm competes on many routes with a rival carrier, East-West (EW), the outcome will depend on how EW reacts to TN's choice. A tree diagram of the situation follows. (Payoffs in million dollars of revenue per week.)

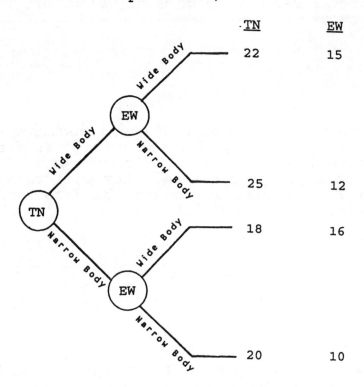

	TN	EW
	22	15
	25	12
	18	16
	20	10

a.   Does the rival firm, EW, have a dominant strategy? If so, what is it? If not, why not?

b.   Use an inductive process to determine what the outcome will be, that is, if one can be determined. Explain.

Information, Incentives, and Contracting

5.   You have bought a franchise for Spudduckers, a fast-food restaurant that specializes in "decorated" baked potatoes. Your

franchise contract calls for you to pay a royalty equal to 20 percent of sales revenue to the franchising company. You estimate demand for the spuds, on a daily basis, to be given by the equation Q = 30,000 - 5,000P. Average variable cost of the spuds is $0.90.

a. Determine your profit-maximizing price for the spuds and the quantity sold at that price. (Disregard any additional revenues from drink sales, etc.)

b. You are in California, and your franchisor can tell you what price to charge for the spuds. In fact, based on the same data you have, the franchisor tells you to set a price of $3.00 per spud. How will this impact your profit? How will it impact the franchisor's profit? Explain.

6. You work at home as a joke writer for a late-night talk show host. Your jokes, and those of other writers, are submitted to a pool from which the host, along with the show's producer and director, pick the ones they will use on the show. You are paid a flat salary plus a commission of $200 for each joke used on the show. They use about one in five of your jokes, and your joke production depends on your time spent thinking them up and writing them on your PC. The more hours you put in, the harder it is for you to come up with something funny, and the more disagreeable the additional work becomes. Your joke production for a typical week is shown in the following table.

Hours Worked	Total Jokes Produced
20	20
30	30
40	38
50	44
60	48

a.   You have had an economics course, so you focus on the
     opportunity cost (forgone shopping, tennis, jogging,
     and sleep, among other things) that occurs as your hours
     worked on producing jokes increases. Your subjective
     evaluation is that if you work on jokes from 20 to 30
     hours per week, the opportunity cost per hour worked is
     $30. From 30 to 40 hours per week, it is $35. From 40
     to 50 hours per week, it increases to $50, and from 50-
     60 hours per week it is $60. How many jokes will you
     submit per week? How did you arrive at this number?

b.   Suppose the show's executives wanted you to submit anoth-
     er ten jokes per week above the number you considered
     optimal. How could they alter the commission schedule
     to get you to do that?

MULTIPLE CHOICE
     Circle the letter that corresponds to the best answer.

1.   A one-shot game is also called:
     (a)   a multi-period sequential game;
     (b)   an infinitely repeated game;
     (c)   a non-sequitur game;
     (d)   a single-period, simultaneous-move game.

2.   Aljomommo Corporation has decided to double its advertising
     regardless of what advertising decision its arch-rival, Sarco,
     chooses. Thus, Aljomommo has:
     (a)   a Nash equilibrium;
     (b)   search costs;
     (c)   a dominant strategy;
     (d)   engaged in a cooperative game.

3.   A game in extensive form:
     (a)   takes that name because it takes a long time to play;
     (b)   can be examined using a game tree diagram with nodes
           and branches;
     (c)   is the only type of game that results in a Nash equili-
           brium;
     (d)   always has more than two players.

4.   After renting a sports car with full insurance coverage, Tammy
     decides to drive recklessly. This is an example of:
     (a)   moral hazard;
     (b)   a one-shot game;
     (c)   a principal-agent problem;
     (d)   signalling.

5.   The reason a consumer will spend a lot more time searching
     for a better deal on a car than searching for a better deal
     on a pair of shoes is that:
     (a)   a good deal on a car is harder to find than a good deal
           on a pair of shoes;
     (b)   there is a lot more difference in cars than there is in
           shoes;
     (c)   cars are more of a necessity than are shoes;
     (d)   the marginal benefit from searching is likely to be much
           higher for cars than for shoes.

Chapter 10

HAND-IN PROBLEMS

Name_____

Course No. and Section_____

Problem 1.

Two high-volume electronics retailers, Bargain Boys and Hitec City will, as in many past years, have Labor Day super sales. However, both are considering TV advertising blitzes in addition to the usual newspaper advertising they do on Labor Day weekend. Each firm will have only one opportunity to make a choice, and they will *not* choose in sequence. Their payoffs in terms of additional third-quarter sales revenues in millions of dollars are shown in the following data.

	Hitec City			
	No TV Ad Blitz		TV Ad Blitz	
No TV AD Blitz	4.5	5.5	*B* 5.5	5.0
Bargain Boys				
TV Ad Blitz	*B* 7.0	*H* 6.6	6.0	*H* 6.1

a.   What type of game is illustrated here?

b.   Examine the payoff table, and search for dominant strategies. Do you find any? Explain.

c.   What will be the outcome of this game?

Chapter 10

HAND-IN PROBLEMS

Name_____

Course No. and Section_____

Problem 2.

Two nationwide players in the used car superstore business, Car Country and Auto Giant, have seen their sales lag because of very long warranties offered with the purchase of new cars. The two firms have been offering 1-year warranties on the cars they sell. To be competitive with new car sellers, they both believe that they must consider a 5-year warranty program on their used cars. The table below shows the payoffs for this game. Both firms will have only one opportunity to make a strategic decision, and they will move simultaneously.

	Auto Giant			
	1-Year Warranty		5-Year Warranty	
1-Year Warranty	15	35	23	40
5-Year Warranty	20	30	18	45

Car Country

a.   Is there a dominant strategy for Car Country? What about Auto Giant?

b.   Determine the outcome of this game, and explain why it will occur.

Chapter 10

HAND-IN PROBLEMS

Name_____

Course No. and Section_____

Problem 3.

Two major regional communications firms, Certified Digi-Serv (CDS) and Double-Time Cable (DTC) are considering bundling cable TV, phone, and high-speed internet service in a "bargain" package. Their choices are to bundle or not to bundle, and CDS is the larger firm and will make the first move. The game is sequential, and a game tree follows.

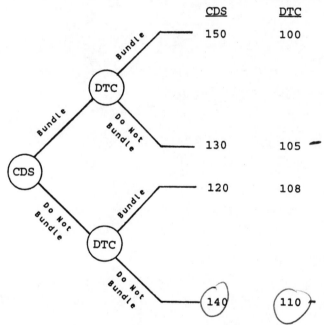

a.   What is the procedure used to determine the strategic choices made in a sequential game of this type?

b.   What will be the outcome of this game? Explain how you can tell.

CHAPTER 11: Topics in
Pricing and Profit Analysis

Programmed Review

This chapter deals with multi-product and multi-market pricing and with revenue- and profit-enhancing strategies the firm may employ in a variety of special circumstances. In some industries goods are priced according to a rule of thumb regarding the margin between the selling price and the cost of goods sold. This margin is called a _____. For any good, the markup may be stated either as a percentage of the _____ _____ or as a percentage of the cost of _____ sold. The former type of markup is called a markup on _____ and the second a markup on _____. An accurate estimate of the price elasticity of _____ will allow management to determine the markup that will be consistent with _____ maximization.

markup

sales price

goods

price

cost

demand

profit

When the firm uses a production process that always results in the output of more than one product, the products are called _____ products. If two such products are produced in fixed proportions but demand for the goods is dissimilar, the firm may end up with _____ production of one of the two goods. The quantity sold of this good will be determined by the point where its marginal revenues is _____.

joint

excess

zero

If one division of a two-division firm sells an input to the other, management faces a problem of _____ pricing. If the external market for the transfer product (input) is perfectly competitive, the _____ price will be the price that should be charged for the internal transfer of that good. If the transfer product division

transfer

market

produces more output than the final product division wishes to buy, there is _____ internal supply of the transfer product. The quantity produced of the final product will be determined where the _____ _____ revenue of that product equals the _____ of the transfer product.

excess

net marginal
price

If a firm produces only one product but sells it in two markets, it may have an opportunity to profit from _____ discrimination. This means it will charge each set of buyers a different price. To be successful in applying two-market price discrimination, the firm must face two markets that have different _____ of demand and can be kept apart. If discrimination is feasible, the firm will charge a higher price in the market where buyers have the _____ elasticity of demand.

price

elasticities

lowest

A firm may use two-part pricing to increase its revenue and profit by charging consumers both a price per unit and an _____ ___. It may also use a strategy of offering "package deals" on related products, a practice called _____.

access fee

bundling

As indicated in the introductory chapter of the text, a firm may choose not to maximize profit. Because of separation of ownership and control, managers may perceive that their salaries depend more on _____ than on profit. If this is true, they may choose a sales quantity that is _____ than the profit-maximizing one, subject, of course, to attaining a profit level that is _____ to shareholders. In addition to the pricing models already reviewed, this chapter illustrates the sales maximization model.

sales

greater

satisfactory

PRACTICE PROBLEMS

Problem on Markup Pricing (ref. EOCQ 1, 2)

1. Jarco, Inc. buys tennis court color surfacer at manufactur-
    er's cost plus 20 percent and sells the material to tennis
    court building contractors. The maufacturer's current cost
    of the surfacer is $140 per 30-gallon drum. If Jarco's per-
    unit handling costs are constant at $4.00 per barrel and its
    current estimate of the elasticity of demand for the product
    in the building contractor market is -3.5, what will be the
    dollar amount of markup that will maximize profit from sales
    of the surfacer?

Problems on Joint Products (ref. EOCP 1, 2, 4, C1, C3, C5)

2. Suppose a firm produces two products, A and B, using a
    single production process. Their product transformation
    curve is shown below.

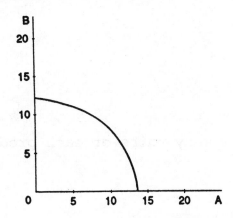

    a. If A and B sell for exactly the same price, what com-
       bination of output will maximize the firm's profit?

    b. If the firm's total cost falls, what will be the effect
       on the transformation curve in the diagram?

Getting Started:
Remember that the transformation curve is based on given costs and that the slope of the isorevenue curve is related to the sales prices of the two products.

3. American Astrotronics Corp. (AAC) makes fur muffs from raccoon skins. Every time it makes a muff, it also obtains one raccoon tail that it can sell to auto specialty companies. The latter market the tails to old car buffs who put them on their antennas for ornamentation. AAC has estimated the demand for fur muffs to be:

$Q_m = 62,000 - 2,000P_m$, so that $MR_m = 31 - 0.001Q_m$.

For raccoon tails, its estimate of demand is:

$Q_t = 40,000 - 2,500P_t$, so that $MR_t = 16 - 0.0008Q_t$.

If the marginal cost curve for the two joint products is:

$MC = 1 + .0002Q$, where Q represents one muff and one tail,

a. How many units of each product should AAC produce?

b. How many units of each product should AAC sell?

c. What price should it charge for each product?

d. If its average cost (SAC) is \$16 at the level of output it produces in (i) above, what will be the firm's economic profit at the prices you have calculated for the two products?

Getting Started:
> The two joint products will always be produced in the same quantity, but if one has negative MR at that quantity, not all of it will be sold. If a solution based on summing the two MR values for the muffs and tails yields negative MR for one good, then the solution will be where the other's MR = MC. The problem immediately below requires the same approach.

THE FOLLOWING PROBLEM REQUIRES CALCULUS

4. Kittydoo Corp. (KC) mines vermiculite, a porous, light-weight mineral. With every ton of vermiculite it mines, it also obtains one ton of potters' clay as a co-product. The vermiculite is sold to household products companies that process and package it as cat litter. The clay is sold to producers of artists' supplies. KC has estimated its monthly demand for vermiculite to be:

$$Q_V = 80,000 - 1,250P_V.$$

For potters' clay, its estimate of monthly demand is:

$$Q_C = 50,000 - 500P_C.$$

If the total cost function for the two products is:

$$TC = 1,500,000 + 2Q + .0002Q^2, \quad \text{where Q represents the joint production of one ton of each product,}$$

a. How many units of each product should KC produce?

b. How many units of each product should KC sell?

   c. What price should it charge for each product?

   d. What will be the firm's economic profit at the
      prices you have calculated for the two products?

Transfer Product Problem   (ref. EOCP 6, C2, C4)

5. Freeway Blaster, Inc. is a firm in Houston that produces
    high-powered car audio systems. Its wholly-owned subsid-
    iary, Coastal Magnetics, is located in Bay City and spe-
    cializes in making equalizer circuits for car audio sys-
    tems. The market for this type of circuit is perfectly
    competitive, and the going wholesale price for a circuit
    is $12. Coastal Magnetics is permitted to do subcontract
    work for other manufacturers of car audio units.
       Freeway Blaster estimates its monthly total cost of
    production of audio systems (<u>not</u> including the equalizer
    circuits) to be represented by the equation below:

$$TC_a = 2,000 + 5Q_a + 0.0105Q_a^2 ,$$

   where Q_a is the number of audio systems produced.

Thus the relevant marginal cost for the systems, without
the cost of the equalizer circuits, is $MC_a = 5 + 0.021Q_a$.

Meanwhile, the monthly total cost function of Coastal
Magnetics is:

$$TC_c \doteq 1,000 + 0.1Q_c + 0.0005Q_c^2,$$

   where Q_c is the number of equalizer circuits produced.

So Coastal's $MC_c = 0.1 + 0.001Q_c$.

If the demand curve facing Freeway Blaster for the audio
units is $Q_a = 10,000 - 50P_a$, giving a marginal revenue
of $MR_a = 200 - 0.04Q_a$,

a. How many audio units should Freeway Blaster sell?

b. What price should Freeway Blaster charge per audio unit?

c. How many equalizer circuits should Coastal Magnetics produce?

d. Should Coastal Magnetics make equalizer circuits for other firms? If so, how many?

Getting Started:

First calculate the net marginal revenue from sales of the final product. Remember that the only remaining cost for the final product division will be what it must spend to get the transfer product. This will determine how much of the final product it is willing to produce. The same approach also applies to the next problem.

Two-Part Pricing Problem   (ref. EOCP 10)

6.   Craggy Jenny's fitness center believes the average custo-
     mer has a demand curve for visits per month given by the
     equation Q = 35 - 5P. Determine the optimal combination
     of price per visit and monthly membership charge if mar-
     ginal cost per visit for Jenny's is $5.

Bundling Problem   (ref. EOCP 9)

7.   Hollyblock Video is considering a plan to market a Snack
     Pack along with its first-run movie rentals. Management
     needs to decide whether to bundle the Snack Packs with
     the movies or to sell them separately. Initial research
     shows that a typical female customer is willing to pay
     up to $3.80 to rent a first-run movie and up to $1.80 to
     buy a Snack Pack. The typical male customer, however,
     will rent a movie for a maximum price of $2.75 but will
     pay up to $3.00 for a Snack Pack. Based on these data,
     what is the firm's best stratgy regarding both bundling
     and pricing?

Price Discrimination Problem   (ref. EOCP 3, 7, C6)

8. Trenchwich Corp. manufactures power trenching machines in the United States. It also sells them in the international market. The company spends a lot of money on lobbying and has been successful in obtaining a high rate of tariff on competing foreign equipment. Trenchwich estimates that the monthly U.S. demand for its machine is given by the following equation:

$$Q_{us} = 3,000 - .2P_{us}, \text{ so that } MR_{us} = 15,000 - 10Q_{us}.$$

Monthly foreign demand for the same machine is given by the equation

$$Q_f = 5,000 - .4P_f, \text{ so that } MR_f = 12,500 - 5Q_f.$$

Trenchwich's total cost function is

$$TC = 200,000 + 800Q, \quad \text{where \$200,000 is monthly fixed cost, and } MC = 800.$$

a. Assuming the firm practices price discrimination, what will be its price per unit in each of the two markets, and how many machines per month will it sell in each market?

b. Calculate the firm's total profit under the above conditions.

Getting Started:
     Applying the usual condition for profit maximization to each of the two markets will get you the solution here.

MULTIPLE CHOICE
Circle the letter that corresponds to the best answer.

1. Nexus Corporation produces two joint products in fixed propor-
    tions. It currently is producing 2000 units of both products,
    where the marginal revenue functions for them are, respec-
    tively, $MR_a = 600 - 0.4Q$ and $MR_b = 400 - 0.03Q$. We can readi-
    ly conclude that:
    (a)   the firm produces too much a and not enough b;
    (b)   it should not sell all of the a it currently produces;
    (c)   it would be logical to sell 2,000 units of each product;
    (d)   the firm should sell no more than 1,500 units of a.

2. In the graphical case depicting two joint products that can
    be produced in variable proportions, a change in the price
    charged for one of the two products will:
    (a)   shift the product transformation curve outward;
    (b)   change the slope of the isorevenue curve;
    (c)   necessarily increase the firm's profit;
    (d)   cause total cost to rise.

3. Welco Corporation has a subsidiary that produces electric
    mini-motors for its line of personal care products. The mini-
    motors are available from many other producers at an invar-
    iable market price of $1.50. It is clear that:
    (a)   Welco's subsidiary should sell mini-motors to other
          firms;
    (b)   the subsidiary should sell mini-motors to Welco at a
          price less than $1.50 or be shut down;
    (c)   Welco will want to buy mini-motors from outside firms;
    (d)   the subsidiary should set its price at $1.50 for sales
          to Welco and for any sales to outside firms.

4. In the analysis of transfer pricing, the term "net marginal
    revenue" is used to:
    (a)   indicate the revenue generated from sales of the transfer
          product to outside firms;
    (b)   indicate the revenue generated by the final product,
          net of all marginal costs but that of the transfer prod-
          uct;
    (c)   determine the network of revenues between inside and
          outside firms;
    (d)   indicate the difference between marginal revenue of the
          transfer product and that of the final product.

Chapter 11.

HAND-IN PROBLEMS

Name_____

Course No. and Section_____

Problem 1.   (show all necessary calculations)

Limbo Turtles, Inc. is a small West Indies firm that raises turtles. Its output consists of two joint products, turtle steaks, which are sold to exotic game restaurants, and turtle shells, which are sold to producers of costume jewelry. Each time Limbo processes a turtle, it obtains one shell and 4 turtle steaks. The shells are sold whole, and the steaks are sold in boxes of 4.

Limbo estimates that the annual demand curve for steaks is $Q_a = 4,400 - 100P_a$ (Q_a is the number of boxes sold), while that for shells is $Q_b = 2,800 - 50P_b$. Thus, the marginal revenue equations for the two products are:

$$MR_a = 44 - 0.02Q_a, \text{ and } MR_b = 56 - 0.04Q_b$$

The firm's annual total cost for the production of the turtles

is given by the equation **TC** = _____, so that
                                    (instructor supplied equation)
MC =_____.
     (instructor supplied equation)

   a. How many boxes of turtle steaks should Limbo Turtles
      produce?

   b. How many turtle shells should Limbo Turtles produce?

(continued next page)

(Ch. 11, Problem 1, continued)

c. How many boxes of turtle steaks should Limbo Turtles <u>sell</u>, and what should be its price per box?

d. How many turtle shells should Limbo <u>sell</u>, and at what price per shell?

e. What will be Limbo's total annual profit?

Chapter 11.

HAND-IN PROBLEMS

Name_____

Course No. and Section_____

Problem 2.

Florida Fabrics, Inc. is a firm in Hoboken, NJ that produces Miami Vice T-shirts. Its wholly-owned subsidiary, West Coast Graphics, is located in Jersey City and specializes in printing designs on T-shirts by the silk screen method. The market for this type of silk screen printing is perfectly competitive, and the going price for printing a shirt is $_____. West Coast Graphics
                              (instructor supplied number)
is permitted to do subcontract work for other manufacturers of T-shirts.

Florida Fabrics estimates its marginal cost of production of shirts (<u>not</u> including the printing) to be represented by the equation below:

$$MC_s = 0.5 + 0.005Q_s \quad \text{where } Q_s \text{ is the number of shirts produced.}$$

Meanwhile, the marginal cost function of West Coast Graphics is:

$$MC_p = 0.10 + 0.0004Q_p, \quad \text{where } Q_p \text{ is the number of shirts printed.}$$

If the demand curve facing Florida Fabrics for the T-shirts is $Q_s = 6,000 - 200P_s$, so that $MR_s = 30 - 0.01Q_s$,

a. How many shirts should Florida Fabrics sell?

b. What price should Florida Fabrics charge per shirt?

(continued next page)

(Chapter 11, Problem 2, continued)

d. How much silk-screen printing should West Coast Graphics do?

e. Should West Coast graphics do printing for other firms? If so, how much?

Chapter 11.

HAND-IN PROBLEMS

Name_____

Course No. and Section_____

Problem 3.

Joytime Matinee Pizza Theater is just an ordinary movie theater that serves pizza at the snack bar. Because of the pizza feature, it does a great business with teenagers who come to see such wonderful movies as Ninja Meets MotheRambo. Owing to its programming and pizza, Joytime knows it can segment the adult ticket market from that for teenagers.

Suppose Joytime's estimate of the weekly demand for adult movie tickets is $Q_a = 1,800 - 200P_a$, giving a marginal revenue in the adult segment of the market of $MR_a = 9 - 0.01Q_a$.

Also, Joytime has estimated teenagers' weekly ticket demand to be $Q_t = 5,600 - 400P_t$, so that $MR_t = 14 - 0.005Q_t$.

If the marginal cost of a ticket for Joytime is $\$$_____:
                                       (instructor supplied number)

    a. Determine the price and quantity sold in each of the two markets.

    b. Calculate the total weekly profit of Joytime if its total cost of supplying tickets on a weekly basis is $TC_t = 16,500 + 2Q$ and the profit contribution per moviegoer from pizza and refreshments is $2.10. Assume all fixed costs are accounted for in the TC_t function.

CHAPTER 12: Factor Markets and Profit-Maximizing Employment of Variable Inputs

Programmed Review

The primary objective of this chapter is to explain how the structure of the market in which a factor (input) is purchased affects the firm's decision regarding the quantity employed of that factor. The change in sales revenue that occurs when the firm employs an additional unit of a given factor is called the marginal _____ _____ of that factor. It can be calculated by multiplying the marginal product of the factor times the _____ _____ from the sale of the output.

revenue

product

marginal revenue

The general rule for profit-maximizing use of a single variable input is to continue to use more of the input until the last unit just _____ for itself. What the input earns the firm is its marginal revenue product, or, in the case of components costs, its _____ marginal revenue product. If the input market is perfectly competitive, the marginal cost to the firm of using an additional unit of it is its _____ _____.

pays

net

market price

If a firm purchases an input in a perfectly competitive market, it will view the supply curve of the input as a _____ line. This is because any amount can be bought for the market price. The same is not true for monopsony, a market where a given firm is the _____ buyer of the input. A monopsony buyer knows that the market supply curve of the input will slope _____ and thus faces rising average and _____ cost for the input. The result is that under monopsony the input earns the firm its net marginal

horizontal

only

upward

marginal

183

_____ product but is paid a _____ amount.   <u>revenue</u> <u>lesser</u>
This occurs because its marginal cost to the firm
exceeds its price.

When a monopoly seller of an input (such as
a labor union) faces off against a monopsony buyer
of the same input, we have a case that is called
_____ bargaining.   Such a case has no   <u>bilateral</u>
determinate solution, a fact which helps to explain why labor negotiations frequently tend to
be lengthy and difficult.

PRACTICE PROBLEMS

Problems on the Profit-Maximizing Employment of One Variable Input
(ref. EOCP 1, 2, 4, 6, 7)

1. Builder's Equipment Co. makes portable cement mixers. Annual revenue and production data for the mixer are given in the table below. The components cost for one mixer is $100. The cost of one worker for one year is $15,000.

    a. Complete the table below.

Quantity of Labor	Quantity of Mixers	Price of one Mixer	Total Revenue	Arc MR	Arc Net Marginal Revenue	Arc MP_L	Arc MRP_L
0	0	$2,000					
10	800	1,920					
20	2,000	1,800					
30	3,500	1,650					
40	5,500	1,450					
50	7,000	1,300					
60	8,000	1,200					
70	8,800	1,120					
80	9,300	1,070					
90	9,500	1,050					

b. What quantity of labor should Builder's employ,
    what level of output should it produce, and what
    price should it charge to maximize profit? WHY?

c. What is the marginal cost of a cement mixer over the
    range from 8,000 to 8,800 mixers per year?

2. Alamo Instruments, Incorporated, manufactures personal
    computers. Demand and labor productivity data per month
    are given in the table below. The components cost per
    computer is $400. The average monthly cost of labor is
    $2,600.

Quantity of Labor	Quantity of Computers	Price	Total Revenue	Arc MR	Arc NMR_L	Arc MP_L	Arc MRP_L	Arc MC of Output
0	0	$2,800						
						10		
5		2,600						
						5		
15		2,400						
						2		
40		2,200						
						2		
65		2,000						
						1.25		
105		1,800						

a. Complete the table.

a.   Complete the table.

b.   What is the profit-maximizing number of computers to be produced monthly, price, and number of workers for Alamo Instruments? WHY?

3.   A manufacturer of sunglasses has productivity and demand data given in the table below (all are in *per hour* terms).

a.   If the hourly cost of one unit of labor is $7 and the components cost of a pair of sunglasses is $1, complete the table below.

Quantity of Output	Quantity of Labor	Price of one Pair Glasses	Total Revenue	Arc MR	Arc Net Marginal Revenue	Arc MP_L	Arc MRP_L
0	0	$20					
100	10	18					
200	15	16					
300	25	14					
400	45	12					
450	57	11					
500	107	10					
550	207	9					

b.   What is the profit-maximizing price, level of output, and quantity of labor for this firm? WHY?

c. Now suppose that the hourly cost of workers for the manufacturer of sunglasses varies according to the following schedule. Complete the table.

Quantity of Labor	Hourly Wage Rate	Total Cost of Labor	Marginal Cost of Labor
0	$ 0		
10	4		
15	5		
25	6		
45	7		
70	8		
120	9		
220	10		

d. Given the information in Part (c), what is the profit-maximizing price, level of output, and quantity of labor for the eyeglass manufacturer?

Problem Relating Input Use to Production Function
    (ref. EOCP C1, C2, C3)

THE FOLLOWING PROBLEM REQUIRES CALCULUS

4. Suppose Banhale Corp. produces product X with the following
    production function:

    $Q_x = K + 5KL - .01KL^2$,   where K is units of capital
                        employed, L is units of labor
                        employed, and Q_x is output.

    a. If the firm faces a fixed product price of $15 per
        unit, has $5 materials cost per unit of X, and is in
        the short run with K fixed at K = 20, what is the
        equation for the marginal revenue product of input L?

    b. Suppose the price of a unit of L is P_L = $40. What
        amount of L will be employed if the firm maximizes
        profit?

    c. What will maximum profit be if the firm's total fixed
        cost is $100,000?

MULTIPLE CHOICE
Circle the letter that corresponds to the best answer.

1. The concept that measures the amount of revenue that an additional unit of a single variable input earns for the firm is the:
    (a) incremental profit contribution;
    (b) variable revenue;
    (c) marginal revenue product;
    (d) wage rate.

2. It will be rational for a firm to use more and more of a single variable input as long as long as what it yields in additional revenue:
    (a) is less than the amount paid for the input;
    (b) exceeds the additional costs associated with using it;
    (c) is greater than its marginal product;
    (d) does not change fixed cost.

3. The concept of net marginal revenue is useful when employment of additional units of an input is always accompanied by:
    (a) components cost;
    (b) wage increases;
    (c) rising fixed costs;
    (d) zero marginal product.

4. A firm purchases labor at a fixed wage of $80 per day and sells its product in a competitive market at an invariable price of $3.20 per unit. If there are no components costs, it should hire an additional worker as long as that worker's marginal product per day is greater than:
    (a) 15 units of output;
    (b) 25 units of output;
    (c) zero;
    (d) 42 units of output.

5. The marginal revenue product of a robot that costs $100 per day, produces 50 units of output per day that sell for $22 each, is installed in a plant with $82,000 per day of fixed costs, and uses $18 worth of components per unit of output produced is:
    (a) $1,840;
    (b) $900;
    (c) $1,100;
    (d) $200.

Chapter 12.

HAND-IN PROBLEMS

Name_____

Course No. & Section_____

Problem 1.

Silver Sails, Inc., manufactures small sailboats. Annual revenue
and production data are given in the table below. The materials
cost for one sailboat is $_____. The annual cost of one unit of
                    (instructor supplied number)
labor is $_____.   Complete the table and find the profit-
          (instructor supplied number)
maximizing quantity of labor, of sailboats, and price of the
sailboats.

Quantity of Labor	Quantity of Sailboats	Price	Total Revenue	Arc MR	Arc NMR_L	Arc MP_L	Arc MRP_L	Arc MC of Output
0	0	$2,000						
20	600	1,900						
30	1,200	1,800						
50	1,800	1,700						
80	2,400	1,600						
120	3,000	1,500						
180	3,600	1,400						
300	4,200	1,300						

Chapter 12.

HAND-IN PROBLEMS

Name

Course No. and Section_____

Problem 2.   **(REQUIRES CALCULUS)**

Suppose a firm has the following production
      function for product X:

$$Q_x = 3KL + 0.225KL^2 - 0.01KL^3.$$

a. If input K is fixed at K = 20, what is the maximum output
   the firm can produce?

(In the rest of the problem, continue to asssume that
input K is fixed at K = 20.)

b. If the firm can sell any amount of product X for **$_____** per
                                        (instructor supplied number)
   unit, what will be the equation for the marginal revenue product
   of input L?

c. What will be the dollar value of MRP_L when it is maximum?

d. How many units of input L will the firm choose to employ if it
   must pay a fixed amount of **$_____** per unit of L to hire
   the input?   **(instructor supplied number)**

CHAPTER 13: Fundamentals of Project Evaluation

Programmed Review

Chapter 13 looks at techniques for analyzing investment opportunities. The process by which a firm's managers determine how to allocate investment expenditures among alternative projects is known as _____ _____.

    capital budgeting

A new undertaking has one-time costs associated with obtaining and organizing the resources necessary to bring it into existence. These costs are called the project _____ or its _____ cost _____.

    price   initial
    outlay

To determine whether or not a project will be profitable, we must compare the present value of its _____ _____, or net _____ _____, with its price.

    net receipts
    cash flows

The present value of a project's net receipts minus its initial cost outlay is equal to its _____ _____ value.

    net present
    value

If the NPV of a project is greater than or equal to zero, the project is _____.

    acceptable

If the net present value of a project is less than zero the project is ____ _____.

    not acceptable

The after-tax value of net operating income plus depreciation for some time period is equal to the _____ _____ _____ for that period.

    net
    cash flow

The process of determining what sum a current dollar amount of money will accumulate to if invested at a certain rate of interest is called _____.

    compounding

The proposition that discounted future amounts are equal to a certain present amount is known as the concept of _____.

    equivalency

The process by which we determine the present value of an amount to be received at some time in the future is called _____, and the interest rate we use in determining present value is called the _____ _____.

    discounting

    discount rate

195

The discount rate that will just equate the present value of the net cash flows to the price of the project is its _____ _____ of _____.   The cost to the firm of obtaining new funds is called the _____ ____ of _____.   This latter value is used in net present value calculations as the _____ _____.   The marginal cost of capital is based on the after-tax cost of new _____ and the expected rate of return on _____.   A firm's optimal capital budget size is determined where its _____ is equal to its _____.   If its IRR is greater than or equal to the MCC, a project is _____.   If its IRR is less than the MCC, a project is not _____.

internal rate
return
marginal cost
capital
discount
rate
debt
equity

IRR   MCC

acceptable
acceptable

Sometimes a firm's capital budget is limited, so that projects which have acceptable NPVs cannot be undertaken.   Therefore, a plan for _____ _____ is necessary.   In this situation, to maximize its profit, a firm will choose from among those sets of projects that meet the capital budget constraint that group of projects whose _____ is _____.

capital
rationing

NPV   greatest

PRACTICE PROBLEMS

Basic Problems on Present Value and Net Present Value
(ref.   EOCP 1-4, 5, 7, 11)

1. You are about to retire. Your firm has given you the choice of receiving a lump sum of $50,000 now or an annuity of $7,500 a year for ten years. Which option is worth more if an interest rate of 6 percent is the appropriate opportunity cost of funds for you? Do not consider income taxes.

2. Lone Star Air Freight, Inc., is trying to determine which of two mutually exclusive airplanes it should purchase. One, a DC-10, costs $3 million and is expected to yield net cash flows of $750,000 for 8 years. The second, a Boeing 727, will require an initial outlay of $2.2 million and is expected to yield net cash flows of $560,000 for 8 years. It is expected that both planes will have a zero salvage value at the end of the eighth year. If the marginal cost of capital is 12 percent, which plane do you recommend that Lone Star purchase? Why?

3. Apache concrete company is considering two mutually
    exclusive batching machine purchases. Machine A costs
    $30,000 and will yield a net cash flow of $5,000 per
    year. Machine B costs $40,000 and will yield a net cash
    flow of $6,500 per year. Both machines have
    expected lives of ten years. The expected salvage value
    of machine A is $2,000 and that of machine B is $3,000.

    a. Compute the net present value of each machine if the
        appropriate cost of capital is 10%.

    b. Which of the two machines should Apache purchase?
        Why?

Net Present Value Problems with a Capital Budget Constraint
(ref. EOCP 6, 8)

4. A group of investors are forming a business partnership.
    They are considering two investments, both of which have
    three-year lives and cost $100,000. Project X has
    expected net cash flows of $47,500 for three years.
    Project Y is expected to have only a net cash flow of
    $165,000 at the end of the third year. The marginal cost
    of capital for the firm is 14 percent.

    a. Find the net present value of each project.

(continued next page)

b. Find the internal rate of return of each project.

c. If the investors have sufficient funds to invest in only one of the two projects which one should they choose? Why?

5. Venture Capital International is considering five possible projects this year. Project A involves the final stages of the development and marketing of a new drug. Project B is the purchase of the rights to and the marketing of a new robot. Project C is the purchase of the rights to and the marketing of a new computer printer. Project D is the purchase of the rights to and marketing a new barbecue sauce, and Project E involves the sale of a new laundry detergent. The initial cost outlays and expected net annual cash flows are shown in the table below.

Project	Project Price	Annual Net Inflows
A	$400,000	$80,000
B	300,000	60,000
C	200,000	50,000
D	200,000	40,000
E	100,000	25,000

Each project has an expected life of twelve years, no anticipated salvage value, and a marginal cost of capital of 15 percent. The firm has a maximum of $500,000 in its capital budget this year.

a. Calculate the NPV of each project.

b. Which of the five projects should VCI undertake? Why?

Problem Involving Calculating the Marginal Cost of Capital (ref. EOCP 9)

6. The Garden of Eden is a large floral and gift shop chain. The company has determined that its optimal capital structure is 30 percent debt financing and 70 percent equity. The current interest rate on new bonds issued by Garden of Eden will be 12 percent, and the company's shareholders expect a return on equity of 18 percent. The company's corporate income tax rate is 35 percent, and interest is a tax deductible expense.

a. What is Garden of Eden's marginal cost of capital?

b. Garden of Eden is considering an investment project with a life of 9 years, a net annual cash flow of $125,000, a salvage value of $10,000, and an initial outlay of $600,000. Would you recommend that Garden of Eden accept this project? Why or why not?

MULTIPLE CHOICE
Circle the letter that corresponds to the best answer.

1.   As applied in the analysis of capital projects, the term "discount rate" means:
     (a)   the percentage difference in project price between the highest and lowest bidders;
     (b)   the interest rate used in determining the present value of the project;
     (c)   the rate at which funds can be obtained from the Federal Reserve;
     (d)   the rate at which project returns are adjusted to account for future inflation.

2.   In capital project analysis, a project is viewed as acceptable when:
     (a)   the rate of discount approaches zero;
     (b)   it has a positive stream of cash flows;
     (c)   its net present value is greater than zero;
     (d)   it has a high internal rate of return.

3.   The after-tax value of operating income plus depreciation for a given time period is that period's:
     (a)   marginal profit;
     (b)   net cash flow;
     (c)   net present value;
     (d)   internal rate of return.

4.   Capital rationing refers to:
     (a)   a system of allocating scarce government loans;
     (b)   the way banks decide who will get capital and who will not;
     (c)   the way a firm allocates operating capital among its subsidiaries;
     (d)   the way a firm with a limited capital budget chooses its best set of projects.

5.   In calculating the present value of a future stream of receipts, one finds that value higher:
     (a)   the higher the discount rate;
     (b)   the lower the discount rate;
     (c)   the shorter the stream of receipts;
     (d)   the farther the initial receipt is from the present.

Chapter 13.

HAND-IN PROBLEMS

Name_____

Course No. and Section_____

Problem 1.

You have just won the grand prize in the American Publishers' House sweepstakes. You have your choice of $10,000,000 now or $750,000 a year for the next 40 years. (You will get the first payment at the end of the first year.) If you accept the $10,000,000 now, you can invest it to yield a _____ percent **(instructor supplied number)** rate of return over the next 40 years. Ignoring any tax consequences of your decision, which alternative should you choose? Why?

Chapter 13.

HAND-IN PROBLEMS

Name_____

Course No. and Section_____

Problem 2.

Sun Coast Sports Centers, Inc., is considering expanding its fitness centers to a new location. The firm will have to raise new capital to expand to the new location. The firm can issue new bonds at a _____ percent rate of interest and shareholders require a _____ percent rate of return on equity **(instructor supplied numbers)**. The company's marginal tax rate is 34 percent, and it has determined that its optimal capital structure is 60 percent debt and 40 percent equity.

  a. Find the marginal cost of capital for Sun Coast Sports.

  b. Opening a new center will require an initial outlay of $500,000. Sun Coast expects that the center will generate net annual cash flows of $75,000 a year for ten years. At the end of ten years Sun Coast believes the new center could be sold to a franchisee for $400,000. Would you recommend that the new facility be built? Why or why not? (Round your answer in part (a) to the nearest whole percent.)

Chapter 13.

HAND-IN PROBLEMS

Name_____

Course No. and Section_____

Problem 3.

Nanoc Corporation is considering acquiring five new product lines this year. The product lines, their initial outlays, their expected annual net cash flows, and their anticipated salvage values based on a ten-year life are shown in the table below. **(Your instructor will supply salvage value numbers.)**

Product	Initial Outlay	Annual Net Cash Flow	Salvage Value
A	$450,000	$90,000	_____
B	350,000	75,000	_____
C	150,000	32,000	_____
D	100,000	20,000	_____
E	50,000	12,000	_____

The firm's marginal cost of capital is 14 percent.

   a. Find the NPV of each of the products.

(continued next page)

b. If Nanoc has a $500,000 limit on its capital budget this
   year, which of these new product lines should be
   acquired? Why?

CHAPTER 14: Risk in Project Analysis
Programmed Review

When there is some doubt regarding the occurrence of its outcome, an investment is characterized as _____. Suppose a person has a choice between an investment whose outcome is a particular dollar amount that is known with certainty and another investment with the same expected dollar return but there is some uncertainty regarding the actual outcome. If a person always chooses the project with the certain outcome, we say the person is _____ _____. If a person always chooses the riskier project, then that individual is a _____ _____. A person who is indifferent between the two alternatives is _____ _____. In discussions of investment project analysis it is usually assumed that the decision makers are _____ _____.

risky

risk averse

risk seeker

risk neutral

risk
averse

We can graphically illustrate the trade-off between risk and return for an investor through the use of _____ curves. For a risk averse person, these curves have a _____ slope, since _____ is considered to be desirable but _____ is undesirable. In other words, a greater _____ is required to compensate for greater risk to leave the investor equally satisfied with the situation.

indifference
positive
return
risk
return

In probability analysis, a possible outcome is called an _____. A numerical value measuring the proportion of times a specific event will occur under a particular set of circumstances is called the _____ of that event. Each event in a listing of all possible outcomes of a given situation is called an _____

event

probability

elementary

209

_____. A group of elementary events is called a _____ _____. When the probability of an event cannot be ascertained either empirically or logically, the analyst must use _____ probabilities.

event

composite event

subjective

To deal with risk in project analysis we compare the expected returns and riskiness of alternative projects. Multiplying each possible outcome of a project by its associated probability and summing these values obtains for us the project's _____ _____. The sum of the squared deviations of each possible outcome from its expected value multiplied by its corresponding probability is the _____ of the returns. The square root of the variance is called the standard _____. The standard deviation is one measure of the _____ of the project.

expected value

variance

deviation

risk

One way of taking risk into account in project analysis is through the discount rate. This method is called the risk-adjusted _____ rate approach. An alternative method is to adjust the expected net cash flow for each time period according to its riskiness. This approach is called the _____ equivalent method.

discount

certainty

PRACTICE PROBLEMS

Basic Problem on Expected Cash Flow and Standard Deviation
(ref. EOCP 2-4)

1. Suppose two one-year projects are expected to have the following returns in relation to the percentage growth in income for a particular region.

% Growth	Net Cash Inflow	
In Income	Project A	Project B
0%	$ 80,000	$ 0
5%	100,000	100,000
10%	120,000	200,000

The firm believes that the following probabilities reflect the chances that each level of income growth will occur.

% Growth in Income	Probability
0%	.25
5%	.50
10%	.25

a. Find the expected value of the net cash flow from each project.

b. Find the standard deviation of the cash flows for each project.

c. Draw rod graphs showing a discrete probability distribution of the net cash flows from each project.

PROJECT A   PROJECT B

d. If the initial outlay required for each of the two projects were $75,000, which one would a risk averse investor accept? Why?

Problem Using Risk-Return Indifference Curves (ref. EOCP 1)

2. Using a set of risk-return indifference curves, show how an investor could prefer an investment with a certain return of $800 to a risky investment with an expected return of $1,200. On the same graph show another risky investment with an expected return of $1,200 that is preferred to the first risky investment with an expected return of $1,200. Assume that the investor is risk averse.

Problem Calculating NPV Using Risk-Adjusted Discount Rates
(ref. EOCP 5, 10)

3. Two business people have four years until retirement. They are considering pooling their funds in one of two investments. The first investment would involve the purchase of manufacturing rights to a designer jean. The second investment would be to buy some undeveloped land and hold it for four years.

    The investors believe that the market for these designer jeans will disappear after four years. The initial cost outlay for the manufacturing rights to the jeans and the necessary equipment is $150,000. The annual operating net cash flows from the jeans are expected to be $75,000. In addition, at the end of four years they expect that the equipment can be sold for $20,000.

    The initial outlay for the land would also be $150,000. The investors expect that the real estate can be sold at the end of four years to net $480,000 after taxes. The risk-adjusted marginal cost of capital for the jeans investment is 18%. The risk-adjusted discount rate for the real estate investment is 24%. Which project should the investors choose?

Problem with Certainty Equivalent Adjustment Factors
(ref.   EOCP 6, 8)

   4.   Complete items <u>a</u> through <u>e</u> below.

   a.   Develop a set of certainty equivalent adjustment factors from the following information on a decision maker's preferences for the expected cash flows from a risky project.

Year	Equivalent Certain Return	Expected Risky Return	Certainty Equivalent Adjustment Factor
1	$ 75,000	$ 80,000	_____
2	90,000	100,000	_____
3	102,000	120,000	_____
4	96,000	120,000	_____
5	90,000	120,000	_____

   b.   Find the present value of the certainty equivalent cash flows using a risk-free discount rate of 8 percent.

   c.   Find the present value of the risky expected cash flows using a risk-adjusted discount rate of 15%.

d. Why do some people argue that the certainty equivalent method of adjusting for risk is superior to the risk-adjusted discount rate method?

e. How could certainty equivalent factors be found that would yield results identical with that of the risk-adjusted discount rate?

MULTIPLE CHOICE
   Circle the letter that corresponds to the best answer.

1.   Suppose a person chooses an investment that is shrouded with uncertainty over one that has the same expected return but is much more of a "sure thing." That person would most likely be described as:
   (a)   a risk averter;
   (b)   someone who is risk neutral;
   (c)   a fiscal conservative;
   (d)   a risk seeker.

2.   The expected value of the net cash flows of a capital project is:
   (a)   its total value, including its contribution to society as a whole;
   (b)   a probability-weighted average of its anticipated cash flows;
   (c)   its net present value before adjusting for risk;
   (d)   the same amount, whether the project is risky or not.

3.   In a risk-return indifference curve map, two points will lie on the same indifference curve if:
   (a)   they represent the same return but are <u>not</u> equally risky;
   (b)   they represent different returns but <u>are</u> equally risky;
   (c)   they are both equivalent to the same certain return;
   (d)   the consumer prefers one point to the other.

4.   An approach to risk analysis that adjusts project inflows themselves rather than the rate at which the inflows are discounted is the:
   (a)   gross present value approach;
   (b)   externality approach;
   (c)   certainty equivalent approach;
   (d)   risk-adjusted flow rate approach.

5.   A risk premium is:
   (a)   the difference between the risk-free discount rate and the risk-adjusted rate;
   (b)   the amount project cost must be inflated to take risk into account;
   (c)   a special charge paid to a firm's insurors when it undertakes a risky project;
   (d)   a round cracker usually eaten with cheese.

Chapter 14.

HAND-IN PROBLEM

Name_____

Course No. and Section_____

Trutza Construction Company is considering two construction projects: a small housing subdivision and a small shopping mall. Both projects are expected to take a year to complete and both would be sold at that time. The net cash flow from either project will depend on the average unemployment rate during the year, as shown below.

% Unemployment	Net Cash Inflows ($1,000s)	
	Mall Project	Housing Project
4%	$200,000	$100,000
6%	160,000	80,000
8%	80,000	50,000
10%	20,000	30,000

Trutza believes that the following probabilities reflect the chances that each level of unemployment will occur. **(The instructor will supply the probability numbers.)**

% Unemployment	Probability
4%	_____
6%	_____
8%	_____
10%	_____

(continued next page)

a. Find the expected value of the net cash inflows from each project.

b. Find the standard deviation of the cash flows from each project.

c. Suppose that the initial outlay for each project is $40 million, payable immediately. Can we now say which project a risk averse investor would choose? Why or why not?

Chapter 15: Economics of Public Sector Decisions

Programmed Review

This chapter deals primarily with managerial decisions concerning the supply of goods and services by the public sector. Goods whose benefits are nondivisible and nonexclusive (people who do not pay for the benefits cannot be excluded from receiving them) are called _____ _____ goods. Benefits from goods that are obtained by third-parties who do not pay for them are called _____ benefits. Much of the output of the public sector consists of goods that are partly public and partly private in nature. These goods are called _____ _____.

All of the explicit and implicit costs of a good borne by its producer make up the _____ cost of a good. The private cost of a good plus any external costs associated with the product make up its _____ cost. The cost, including both private and external costs, of another unit of a good is the _____ _____ cost of the product. Similarly, the private and external benefits of another unit of a good make up its marginal _____ _____. To maximize the social welfare, each good should be produced up to the point where its _____ social _____ is equal to its _____ social _____.

The ratio of the marginal social benefit of a good to its marginal social cost is called its incremental _____ - _____ ratio. No incremental activity should be undertaken when this ratio is less than _____.

pure public

external

mixed goods

private

social

marginal social

social benefit

marginal
benefit marginal
cost

benefit - cost

one

The extension of capital project analysis to public sector microeconomic decisions is called _____ - _____ analysis. In the calculation   cost - benefit
of costs and benefits, items are usually classi-
fied as direct or indirect costs or benefits.
Costs directly associated with a project are its
_____ costs.   Benefits obtained by the   direct
users of a project are _____ benefits.   direct
External, or third-party, benefits and costs are
_____ benefits and costs.   indirect

The rate of discount that, in theory, should be applied to public investment projects is the social _____ of _____. Generally speak-   rate   discount
ing, the higher the discount rate employed, the _____ the present value of the benefit   lower
stream generated by a project. Thus, the choice
of a discount rate is an important one. This
rate should reflect the _____ cost of   opportunity
resources withdrawn from the private sector.

Cost-benefit analysis does have several po-
tential pitfalls connected with its use.   One
problem is that it is difficult to _____   accurately
_____ future benefits and costs. Another   estimate
difficulty is the _____ of gathering information   cost
for cost-benefit analyses.

PRACTICE PROBLEMS

Basic Problem Using Cost-Benefit Analysis (ref. EOCP 2)

1. The city council of Serta is considering building a lake near the city. The lake would provide both a source of city water and recreational facilities. The initial outlay required for the lake is $2,000,000. It is expected to yield net benefits of $280,000 a year for 25 years.

    a. Would you recommend building the lake if the appropriate social rate of discount is 9%? Why or why not?

    b. Would your answer to part (a) change if the social rate of discount were 14 percent? Explain.

Cost-Benefit Problems Involving Several Projects
(ref EOCP 3-7)

2. The city of Marion is considering the following projects as possible items in this year's capital budget. Which would be acceptable from a benefit-cost standpoint if the appropriate social rate of discount is 10 percent?

Project	Project Life (Years)	Annual Differential Benefits	Annual Differential Costs	Initial Capital Outlay
(A) War on Drugs	10	$ 900,000	$300,000	$2,000,000
(B) Expand Sewage Treatment Plant	20	1,250,000	200,000	8,000,000
(C) Low-Income Housing	15	680,000	250,000	3,000,000
(D) Urban Renewal	15	700,000	300,000	3,500,000
(E) New City Hall	20	625,000	150,000	4,000,000
(F) Centennial Celebration	2	330,000	50,000	500,000
(G) Subway System	20	1,400,000	500,000	6,000,000
(H) New Street	10	400,000	200,000	1,000,000

(worksheet for Prob. 2)

3. How would your answer in Problem 1 change if the appropriate social rate of discount were 15 percent?

4. Suppose that the city of Marion (Problem 1) has only
    $8,000,000 in its capital budget for this year. Which of
    the projects listed in Problem 1 should it undertake?
    Why?   (Assume that the social rate of discount is 10
    percent, as in Problem 2.)

5. Cairo City is considering the following capital projects for the next fiscal year.

Project	Initial Capital Outlay	Annual Differential Costs	Annual Differential Benefits
Enlarge Convention Center Arena	$2.00 million	$ 60,000	$500,000
Build a New Park	1.95 million	40,000	450,000
Build a New Fire Station	1.90 million	70,000	600,000
Drainage Project	2.05 million	50,000	500,000
Build Elevated Railway	2.10 million	100,000	650,000

The city has a limited capital budget so that it will be able to fund only one of the projects. If the social rate of discount is 12 percent and the expected life of each project is 10 years, which one should Cairo City choose? Why?

(worksheet for Prob. 5)

MULTIPLE CHOICE
    Circle the letter that corresponds to the best answer.

1.   Which of the following is the best example of a pure public
     good?
     (a)   a rock concert;
     (b)   a toll highway;
     (c)   a national army;
     (d)   a municipal swimming pool.

2.   The difference between the marginal social cost of a good
     and its marginal private cost is:
     (a)   made up of taxes;
     (b)   the revenue the good generates;
     (c)   the amount of its marginal cost that is paid for by the
           government;
     (d)   attributable to externalities.

3.   Suppose the marginal social cost of a good is less than its
     marginal social benefit. This would indicate that:
     (a)   the good is a pure public good;
     (b)   production of the good is less than the socially
           optimal amount;
     (c)   more of the good could be produced without increasing
           total social cost;
     (d)   total social cost is falling and less than total social
           benefit.

4.   In analyzing a public capital project, the most difficult
     components to quantify usually are:
     (a)   the direct costs of the project;
     (b)   the direct benefits of the project;
     (c)   the capital costs of the project;
     (d)   the project's indirect costs and benefits.

5.   A public capital project is acceptable if:
     (a)   it can be bought at a price below that prevailing in
           the private sector for the same project;
     (b)   its marginal social costs equal its marginal social
           benefits;
     (c)   it has a benefit-cost ratio greater than 1.0;
     (d)   it does not have too many indirect benefits or costs.

Chapter 15.

HAND-IN PROBLEM

Name_____

Course No. and Section_____

Sludge Falls is developing its budget for the next fiscal year, and the city is considering the capital projects listed below.

Project	Initial Capital Outlay	Annual Differential Benefits	Annual Differential Costs
Build a Dam	$5.00 million	$750,000	$ 50,000
Enlarge Airport	4.95 million	700,000	75,000
Build a New Library	4.90 million	725,000	90,000
Build New Recreation Centers	5.05 million	680,000	125,000
Beautify Downtown	5.10 million	625,000	80,000

  a. Calculate the benefit-cost ratio for each of these projects if the social rate of discount is _____ percent and the expected life of each project is 20 years. **(The instructor will supply the social rate of discount.)** Which projects are acceptable?

(continued next page)

b. If Sludge Falls can accommodate only one of these
   projects in its capital budget, which one should it
   select? Why?

CHAPTER 16: Legal and Regulatory Environment of the Firm

Programmed Review

This chapter gives an overview of the legal and regulatory environment in which firms operate in the United States. The laws affecting a business firm may be divided into three basic types: the law of _____, _____ law, and the law of _____. The laws that deal with wrongful acts that are viewed as offenses against the state or government are _____ laws. Injuries sustained by private parties because of a wrongful act involving the breach of a duty created by law are _____. The establishment of contractual obligations is covered in the law of _____.

torts criminal contracts

criminal

torts

contracts

The largest volume of tort cases occurs in the area of _____. This term can be defined as the failure to exercise reasonable care in performing a duty created by law. A binding agreement between two or more parties is called a _____. Generally, contracts should be written, although some oral contracts can be binding. The possible remedies for breach of _____ include (1) rescinding the contract, (2) suing for specific performance, and (3) suing for damages.

negligence

contract

contract

Both the federal government and the states have enacted laws to prevent the concentration of economic power. These laws are commonly called _____ laws. Laws intended to prevent deceptive and other unscrupulous business methods are called business _____ laws.

antitrust

practices

The four primary federal antitrust laws are the Sherman Act of 1890, The _____

Clayton

233

Act (1914), the Federal _____ Commission Act (1914), and the _____-Patman Act (1936). Parties injured by violations of the Sherman Act are entitled to _____ damages. Certain acts or practices that are viewed as wrongful "in and of themselves" are called _____ ___ violations of the antitrust laws. These violations include _____ fixing, division of _____, group _____, and _____ agreements.

Trade
Robinson

treble

per se

price   markets
boycotts   tying

A federal agency that takes action outside the courts in matters involving competition and business practices is the Federal _____ Commission. Many other federal regulatory agencies also exist; typically they develop _____and _____ as well as provisions for dealing with parties that _____ these regulations.

Trade

standards rules

violate

Firms in industries where the entire industry output can be produced most efficiently by a single firm are called _____ monopolies. In such cases the government frequently allows a monopoly to exist but sets a ceiling price on the firm's output where P = _____. The firm may also be allowed to use price _____ in the form of _____ pricing. Natural monopolies frequently are found in the public utilities industries (electricity, gas, water).

natural

LAC
discrimination
block

MULTIPLE CHOICE
Circle the letter that corresponds to the best answer.

1. The three <u>basic</u> types of laws affecting business in the United States are:
    (a)   criminal law, fire codes, and antitrust law;
    (b)   the law of contracts, criminal law, and the law of torts;
    (c)   antitrust law, regulatory law, and maritime law;
    (d)   international law, common law, and the antitrust laws.

2. Which of the following laws was enacted primarily to address the problem of discriminatory pricing related to chain stores:
    (a)   the Cellar-Kefauver Act;
    (b)   the Mann Act;
    (c)   the Robinson-Patman Act;
    (d)   the Clayton Act.

3. Under United States federal law, the amount that an injured firm can collect in settlement of antitrust damages is:
    (a)   limited to the actual amount of damages;
    (b)   unlimited;
    (c)   limited to twice the amount of actual damages;
    (d)   specified to be three times actual damages.

4. In an industry characterized by natural monopoly, such as the electric power industry:
    (a)   a firm's marginal cost is likely to be less than its average cost;
    (b)   average cost pricing may cause the firm to incur economic losses;
    (c)   it is not possible for a private firm to generate a normal profit;
    (d)   price discrimination is never permitted.

5. In the 1970s and 80s, backlashes against regulation occurred largely because:
    (a)   too many industries were harmed by price wars;
    (b)   experts argued that regulators had protected established interests in certain industries;
    (c)   major firms in many regulated industries believed deregulation would increase competition;
    (d)   consumer organizations mounted widespread campaigns in favor of deregulation

SOLUTIONS FOR PRACTICE PROBLEMS

AND ANSWERS TO MULTIPLE CHOICE QUESTIONS

CHAPTER 1:

1. The important points are (a) that General Motors (GM), as well as many other U.S. and foreign corporate giants, has become a player in a global, rather than simply a national, market and (b) GM's decision making has become more complex as the world economy has become more integrated. GM's entry into Europe occurred decades ago.   However, its European divisions generally have not had great success in selling their vehicles in markets outside Europe. Fiat, although plagued by losses, is a large European producer, and GM is worried, no doubt, that someone else will take it over, turn it around, and gain market share in Europe. In today's world, GM simply cannot ignore the fate of rival firms located outside the U.S.

Problems Relating to Value of the Firm

2. To determine the present value of the two profit streams, divide the expected profit for each year by $(1.06)^t$, where t = 1 for 2004, 2 for 2005, etc., as shown in the second column below. The results appear in the third and fourth columns.

Year	$(1.06)^t$	Present Value of Profit of CB	Present Value of Profit of SH
2004	1.06	$1,132,075	$1,698,113
2005	1.1236	1,156,995	1,690,993
2006	1.1910	1,679,261	1,595,298
2007	1.2625	1,663,366	1,504,950
2008	1.3382	1,643,999	1,569,272
Sum of present values:		$ 7,275,696	$ 8,058,626

a. Ms. Smyth should reject the stockbroker's advice.

b. Given Ms. Smyth's time horizon, the present value of SH's stream of expected profits exceeds that of CB by the amount $8,058,626 - 7,275,696, or $782,930. Even though CB's expected profit is higher in three of the five years, those years are farther in the future than the years when SH has profits greater than CB's. Far off returns are less valuable than returns that occur soon, so the five-year stream of SH turns out to be the most valuable one. It has a present value that is over 10 percent higher than that of CB, and that should have a positive impact on the stock appreciation of SH as compared to that of CB.

3. If SH lowers its home prices (assuming CB's prices do not
    change), consistent with the law of demand, it can expect the
    quantity demanded of its homes to increase. Of course, it
    will then sell *more* homes but at lower prices per home. Note
    that this assumes that the determinants of demand for its
    homes do not change. One of those is the price of CB's homes,
    and it may be an unwarranted assumption that CB will not
    change its prices. Regarding the profits of SH, even assuming
    that CB does not change its prices, we do not have enough
    information to determine whether price cutting by SH will
    improve its own profits. This will depend on *how much* buyers
    respond to the lower prices, something we will examine in
    detail in Chapter 2. Finally, if the price cutting does grow
    SH profits, but the growth takes a number of years, the far
    off returns will be worth less than nearer ones, so the result
    for SH could be a stream similar to the one we had for CB, and
    that had a lower present value than the original SH stream.

Problems On Basic Demand and Supply Analysis

4. a. P_2 is the equilibrium price, since quantity demanded and
        quantity supplied would be the same at P_2.

    b. At P_1, quantity demanded exceeds quantity supplied. There
        is a shortage, so price will rise.

    c. At P_3, quantity supplied exceeds quantity demanded. There
        is a surplus, so price will fall.

    d. Demand for eyeglasses will decrease, since the surgery is
        a substitute for them. The demand curve in the diagram
        will shift to the left, and price will fall.

    e. Because of the impact on cost of production, supply will
        decrease. The supply curve in the diagram will shift to
        the left, and price will rise.

5. The completed table follows.

Price Per Lb. In Cents	Quantity Demanded	Quantity Supplied	$(Q_s - Q_d)$
90	200	1,700	1,500
80	400	1,400	1,000
70	600	1,100	500
60	800	800	0
50	1,000	500	-500
40	1,200	200	-1,000

a.   The equilibrium price of pears is 60 cents, because that price equates quantity supplied with quantity demanded.

b. $(Q_s - Q_d)$ has been completed above.

c.   A positive number in the column $(Q_s - Q_d)$ indicates that there is a surplus. A negative number corresponds to a shortage.

d.   If price were at 70 cents per lb., there would be a surplus of 500 units and price would eventually fall.

6.   The easy way to approach this problem is to let quantity demanded equal quantity supplied, and solve for the equilibrium price. Then, any price above the equilibrium one will result in a surplus, while prices below equilibrium will result in a shortage. So,

4,000,000 - 10,000P = -1,000,000 + 40,000P, and, adding

1,000,000 + 10,000P to each side of the equation,

5,000,000 = 50,000P. Thus, P = 5,000,000/50,000 = **100**.

a.   At P = $180, there will be a surplus, since 180 > 100. Substituting P = 180 into the equations for the supply curve and the demand curve, we determine that the surplus is $(Q_s - Q_d)$ = 6,200,000 - 2,200,000 = **4,000,000**.

b.   As calculated above, yes, $100 is the equilibrium price, since that is where quantity demanded equals quantity supplied. (Both are equal to 3,000,000.)

Multiple Choice Questions

1. **(c)**; 2. **(d)**; 3. **(c)**; 4. **(a)**; 5. **(a)**.

CHAPTER 2: Solutions for Practice Problems

Basic Problems on Demand and Revenue

1. a) Completed table:

Price (P)	Quantity Demanded (Q)	Total Revenue (TR)	Arc Marginal Revenue (MR)
16	0	0	
			14
14	10	140	
			10
12	20	240	
			6
10	30	300	
			2
8	40	320	
			-2
6	50	300	
			-6
4	60	240	
			-10
2	70	140	
			-14
0	80	0	

b)   Your graphs should look like those on the next page.

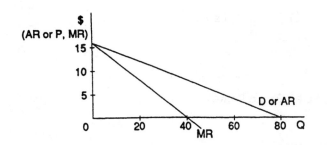

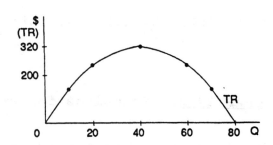

2. Since elasticity is percent change in quantity divided by percent change in price, we have:

$$E = \frac{\frac{\Delta Q}{Q}}{\frac{\Delta P}{P}} = \frac{\Delta Q}{\Delta P} \cdot \frac{P}{Q} = \frac{Q_2 - Q_1}{P_2 - P_1} \cdot \frac{P_2 + P_1}{Q_2 + Q_1}$$

3. Completed table:

	Total Revenue (TR)	Quantity Demanded (Q)	Price (P)
Arc MR			
	0	0	115
110			
	550	5	110
100			
	1050	10	105
90			
	1500	15	100
80			
	1900	20	95
70			
	2250	25	90
60			
	2550	30	85

a. Demand is elastic throughout the table since MR never gets into the negative range.

b.
$$E = \frac{5}{-5} \cdot \frac{185}{45} = \frac{-185}{45} = \underline{\underline{-4.11}}$$

4. If $Q_X = 800 - 25P_X$, then

a. Adding $25P_X$ and subtracting Q_X from each side of the above equation yields

$$25P_X = 800 - Q_X.$$

Now divide both sides by 25 to get

$$\underline{\underline{P_X = 32 - .04Q_X = AR.}}$$

b. $TR = Q_X(P_X) = Q_X(32 - .04Q_X) = \underline{\underline{32Q_X - .04Q_X^2.}}$

MR has the same intercept as AR but twice the negative slope, so MR = $32 - .08Q_X$.

c. At the mid-point of the demand curve, MR = 0, so Q = 400. From the P_X equation, price is 16 when quantity is 400, so TR = 16(400) = $\underline{\$6,400}$.

Word Problems Using Arc Elasticity

5. a.
$$-2 = \frac{Q_2 - 12,000}{-.1} \cdot \frac{0.8}{Q_2 + 12,000} ;$$

$.8Q_2 - 9,600 = .2Q_2 + 2,400 ;$ $.6Q_2 = 12,000 ;$

$$Q_2 = \underline{\underline{20,000}}$$

b. $TR_1 = .45(12,000) = 5,400 ;$ $TR_2 = .35(20,000) = \underline{\underline{7,000}}$

Increase in TR = 7,000 - 5,400 = $\underline{\underline{\$1,600}}$

6. a.
$$-1.5 = \frac{2,000 - 1,200}{P_2 - 8.40} \cdot \frac{P_2 + 8.40}{2,000 + 1,200} ;$$

$800P_2 + 6,720 = -4,800P_2 + 40,320 ;$ $5,600P_2 = 33,600 ;$

$$P_2 = \underline{\underline{\$6.00}}$$

b. $TR_1 = 8.40(1,200) = 10,080 ;$ $TR_2 = 6.00(2,000) = 12,000.$

Increase in TR = $\underline{\$1,920}$

c.

$$1.20 = \frac{Q_2 - 2,400}{6 - 8.40} \cdot \frac{6 + 8.40}{Q_2 + 2,400} \; ;$$

$$14.40 \; Q_2 - 34,560 = -2.88Q_2 - 6,912 \; ; \quad 17.28Q_2 = 27,648 \; ;$$

$$Q_2 = \underline{1,600}$$

CALCULUS PROBLEMS

Demand Function Problems

7. a. $Q_X = 260 - 10P_X - 400 + 480 = \underline{340 - 10P_X}$

    b. $E = -10 \cdot \dfrac{24}{100} = -\underline{2.4}$

    c. $E_{XY} = \dfrac{80 - 100}{210 - 200} \cdot \dfrac{210 + 200}{80 + 100} = -\underline{4.56}$

8. a. $Q = 120 - 200 - 12 + 270 = \underline{178}$

    TR = 178(100) = $\underline{\$17,800}$

    b. $E = -2 \times 100/178 = -\underline{1.12}$

    c. Complements; an increase in the price of dinners results in a decrease in the quantity of pets sold.

    d. $E_I = .15 \times 1,800/178 = \underline{1.52}$

Equation Using the Demand Curve

9. a. $5P_X = 4,500 - Q_X; \quad P_X = \underline{\underline{AR}} = \underline{900 - .2Q_X}$

    $$\underline{\underline{TR}} = P_X(Q_X) = (900 - .2Q_X)(Q_X) = \underline{900Q_X - .2Q_X^2}$$

    $$\underline{\underline{MR}} = \frac{dTR}{dQ} = \underline{900 - .4Q_X}$$

    b. Where MR = 0 = 900 - .4Q_X ; $Q_X = \underline{2,250}$

    $P_X = \underline{450}$

    c. 450(2,250) = $\underline{1,012,500}$

Multiple Choice Questions

1. (a);   2. (a);   3. (b);   4. (c);   5. (a);   6. (d).

CHAPTER 3:   Solutions for Practice Problems

Problems on Estimated Demand Functions

1.

a.   In the equation, 800 is the intercept term. The coefficient of P_x, -2.5, indicates that a price increase of $1 will lead to a reduction in quantity sold of 2.5 units. The negative sign on P_x indicates that the demand curve for X slopes downward to the right. The coefficient of P_y, -50, indicates that X and Y are complements and that a $1 increase in P_y will cause Q_x to fall by 50 units. The coefficient of P_z, +4, indicates that Z is a substitute for X and that a $1 increase in P_z will lead to a four-unit increase in quantity sold of X. The coefficient of income, +.01. indicates that X is a normal good and that a $1 increase in income will increase Q_x by .01 of a unit.

The R^2 of 0.89 indicates that 89 percent of the variation in the dependent variable, Q_x, is "explained" by the regression model.

b.   i)   With the given values, we have

$$Q_x = 800 - 2.5P_x - 50(20) + 4(125) + .01(10,000)$$

$$= \underline{\underline{400 - 2.5P_x}}.$$

ii)   From the above, $P = 160 - 0.4Q_x$, and
$MR = 160 - 0.8Q_x$.   Where MR = 0,

$160 - 0.8Q_x = 0$; $Q_x = \underline{200}$.
Thus, P will be $\underline{80}$ and maximum TR = $\underline{\underline{\$16,000}}$.

iii) With $P_x = \$100$,

$$e_{px} = -2.5(P_x/Q_x) = -2.5\ (100/150) = \underline{\underline{-1.67}}.$$

(Note that -2.5 is the coefficient of P_x and ia also
the partial derivative of the Q_x function
with respect to P_x.)

2.

    a.   Given the demand function equation and the values of the independent variables we have:

$$Q_{mwj} = 2000(0.36 \text{ x } 3.53 \text{ x } 0.57 \text{ x } 0.55)$$

$$= 2000(0.4) = \underline{800}.$$

    b.   In this power function, the exponent of each independent variable is the elasticity of quantity with respect to that variable. Thus Q_{mwj} has an elasticity of -2.5 with respect to its own price, an elasticity of +4.2 with respect to the substitute burgers, an elasticity of +0.8 with respect to corn meal mush, and an income elasticity of -0.1. The latter indicates that McWhopperjaws are an inferior good.

MULTIPLE CHOICE QUESTIONS

1. (**a**); 2. (**c**); 3. (**a**); 4. (**b**).

CHAPTER 4

MULTIPLE CHOICE QUESTIONS

1. (**d**); 2. (**a**); 3. (**d**); 4. (**a**); 5. (**b**).

CHAPTER 5: Solutions for Practice Problems

Problems on Long-Run Least Cost Combination of Inputs

    1.   Let MP_s = marginal product of one stencil and MP_m = marginal product of the machine. Then we have

$$\frac{MP_s}{P_s} < \frac{MP_m}{P_m} \text{ , or } \frac{6}{24} < \frac{150}{450} \text{ , or } .25 < .33.$$

Since the marginal product per \$1 spent on a stencil is less than that per \$1 spent on the machine, our initial reaction is that Joe should buy the machine. Other considerations are whether Joe has enough business to warrant having the machine, whether he will lose flexibility by having the machine instead of more stencils (he could send the stencils to more than one job), and whether the machine will reduce the use of other inputs such as labor.

2. A least cost combination of inputs requires that

$$\frac{MP_K}{P_K} = \frac{MP_L}{P_L} \ .$$

Here, P_K per hour = \$6,000/[260 x 8] = \$6,000/2,080 = \$2.88. Since the tortilla machine will require one worker to run it, we must figure the cost of one machine plus one worker on a per hour basis. Thus $P_{K \& L}$ = \$2.88 + 4.00 = \$6.88. The hourly cost of one worker plus a hand press, $P_{L \& HP}$ = \$4.00 + .01 = \$4.01.

In this case,

$$\frac{MP_{K \& L}}{P_{K \& L}} = \frac{1,000 \text{ tortillas}}{\$6.88} = 145.3 \text{ tortillas per } \$1.$$

Also,

$$\frac{MP_{L \& HP}}{P_{L \& HP}} = \frac{200 \text{ tortillas}}{\$4.01} = 49.9 \text{ tortillas per } \$1.$$

Thus, the marginal product per additional \$1 spent is greater for the automated tortilla press than for the worker with the hand press. Therefore, La Venganza should use the automated press.

Alternatively,

$$\frac{P_{K \& L}}{MP_{K \& L}} = \frac{\$6.88}{1,000 \text{ tortillas}} = \$.007 \text{ per tortilla, and}$$

$$\frac{P_{L \& HP}}{MP_{L \& HP}} = \frac{\$4.01}{200 \text{ tortillas}} = \$.02 \text{ per tortilla.}$$

Therefore, the marginal cost of another tortilla is lower with the automated press.

3. A least cost combination of inputs requires that

$$\frac{MP_K}{P_K} = \frac{MP_L}{P_L} \;.$$

In this case, on a *per day* basis,

$$\frac{MP_K}{P_K} = \frac{400 \text{ ft.}}{\$196} = 2.04 \text{ ft. per } \$1, \text{ and}$$

$$\frac{MP_L}{P_L} = \frac{160 \text{ ft.}}{\$144} = 1.11 \text{ ft. per } \$1.$$

Thus, the marginal product per additional $1 spent is greater for the jackhammer than it is for the third worker. Therefore, the sprinkler company should use the jackhammer instead of the third worker.

Alternatively,

$$\frac{P_K}{MP_K} = \frac{\$196}{400 \text{ ft.}} = \$.49 \text{ per ft., and}$$

$$\frac{P_L}{MP_L} = \frac{\$144}{160 \text{ ft.}} = \$.90 \text{ per ft.}$$

Therefore, the marginal cost of laying another foot of sprinkler pipe is lower with the jackhammer.

4. a. With input b fixed at b = 3, the average and marginal products of a are the following:

a	Q = Output	AP_a	MP_a
1	86	86.00	
2	145	72.50	59
3	197	65.67	52
4	245	61.25	48
5	289	57.80	44
6	331	55.17	42

b. With input a fixed at a = 2, the average and marginal
    products of b are the following:

b	Q = Output	AP_b	MP_b
1	84	84.00	
			35
2	119	59.50	
			26
3	145	48.33	
			23
4	168	42.00	
			22
5	190	38.00	
			15
6	205	34.17	

c. No, since the marginal product of $1 spent on a
    exceeds that of $1 spent on b, or

$$\frac{MP_a}{P_a} > \frac{MP_b}{P_b}, \text{ or } \frac{52}{40} > \frac{23}{42}, \text{ or } 1.3 > .55.$$

d. Increasing returns to scale, since a doubling of inputs
    more than doubles output.

Problems on Short-Run Product of a Variable Input

5. a. AP_L = 500/10 = 50.

    b. AP_L will be maximum at L = 15, since this is where the
        ray from the origin is tangent to the curve.
        The value of AP_L will be 1200/15 = 80.

    c.

L	Q = Output	MP_L
0	0	
		40
5	200	
		60
10	500	
		140
15	1200	
		30
25	1500	

    d. The basic point is that when MP_L > AP_L, AP_L will rise,
        but MP_L < AP_L causes AP_L to fall. When L = 5, AP_L = 40,
        but between L= 5 and L = 10 MP_L = 60, so AP_L rises (to
        50 at L = 10). From L = 15 to L = 25, the MP_L is only

30; this causes the AP_L, which was 80 at L = 15 to fall to 1500/25 = 60 at L = 25.

6. The completed table appears below.

Units of z	TP_z	AP_z	MP_z
0	0	- - -	
			100
2	200	100	
			200
4	600	150	
			150
6	900	150	
			102
8	1,104	138	
			73
10	1,250	125	

Relation of Short-Run Total Product Function to Per Unit Product Functions

7.   a) $MP_L = 45 + 12L - L^2$

     b) $AP_L = 45 + 6L - \frac{1}{3}L^2$

     c)   Marginal product will be zero when TP is maximized. Therefore,

          $45 + 12L - L^2 = 0$; $(-L + 15)(L + 3) = 0$;   L = 15

          Q = 675 + 1350 - 1125 = $\underline{900}$

d) This occurs where the <u>derivative</u> of MP_L = 0, or

$$\frac{dMP_L}{dL} = 0 = 12 - 2L; \quad L = \underline{6}$$

e) This occurs where the derivative of AP_L = 0, or

$$\frac{dAP_L}{dL} = 0 = 6 - \frac{2}{3}L; \quad L = \underline{9}$$

$$AP_L = 45 + 54 - 27 = \underline{\underline{72}}$$

MULTIPLE CHOICE QUESTIONS

  1. (**a**); 2. (**a**); 3. (**c**); 4. (**d**); 5. (**b**).

CHAPTER 6: Solutions for Practice Problems.

Tabular Problems on Cost of Production

  1. The completed table follows.

MP	L	Q	STC	AFC	AVC	TVC	MC
	0	0	200	---	---	0	
4							12.50
	5	20	450	10	12.50	250	
8							6.25
	10	60	700	3.33	8.33	500	
6							8.33
	15	90	950	2.22	8.33	750	
4							12.50
	20	110	1200	1.82	9.09	1000	
3							16.67
	25	125	1450	1.60	10.00	1250	
2							25.00
	30	135	1700	1.48	11.11	1500	
1							50.00
	35	140	1950	1.43	12.50	1750	

2. Your filled-in table should look like this:

SMC	MP$_b$	Output of X	Input of b	AP$_b$	AVC	STC
		0	0	---	0	120
1.76	17					
		17	1	17.00	1.76	150
4.29	7					
		24	2	12.00	2.50	180
5.00	6					
		30	3	10.00	3.00	210
6.00	5					
		35	4	8.75	3.43	240
7.50	4					
		39	5	7.80	3.85	270
10.00	3					
		42	6	7.00	4.29	300

Relation of Expansion Path to Long-Run Average Cost

3. a) Your cost curve should look like this:

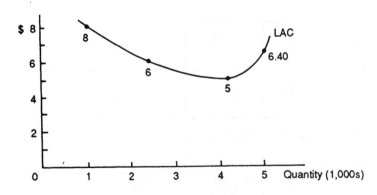

b) The MRTS will have the same value at all points on the
expansion path, and this value will equal the ratio of
the price of L to that of K, or 60/80 = 0.75.

c) Since the LAC curve is U-shaped, the LMC will be below
it as it falls, above it as it rises, and will pass
through the minimum of LAC.

Relation of Total Product to Variable Cost

4. a) 30; b) 500; c) $1.60; d) 20, 20; e) $1250, $2.50

CALCULUS PROBLEMS

Relation of Short-Run Total Cost to Per Unit Functions

5. a) $AVC = 40 - 0.5Q + 0.02Q^2$

   b) $SMC = dSTC/dQ = 40 - Q + 0.06Q^2$

   c) $AFC = 2,000/Q$

   d) $SAC = 2000/Q + 40 - 0.5Q + 0.02Q^2$

   e) $SAC = 100 + 40 - 10 + 8 = \underline{138}$

   f) $AFC = 2000/40 = \underline{50}$

   g) $dAVC/dQ = 0 = -0.5 + 0.04Q;\quad Q = \underline{12.5}$

6. a) $AFC = 500/Q = 500/20 = \underline{25}$

   b) $MC = 40 - 3Q + 0.12Q^2;\quad dMC/dQ = 0 = -3 + 0.24Q;$
   $Q = \underline{12.5}$

   c) $AVC = 40 - 1.5Q + 0.04Q^2;\quad dAVC/dQ = 0 = -1.5 + 0.08Q;$
   $Q = 18.75;\quad AVC = 40 - 28.13 + 14.06 = \underline{25.93}$

MULTIPLE CHOICE QUESTIONS

   1. (c); 2. (d); 3. (b); 4. (d); 5. (a).

CHAPTER 7: Solutions for Practice Problems

Tabular Problems on the Profit-Maximizing Level of Output

1.
   a. The completed table appears on the following page.

Q	P	TR	MR	MC	Mπ	TVC
0	$30	$ 0				$ 0
			$27	$25	$ 2	
1	27	27				25
			24	20	4	
3	25	75				65
			20	16	4	
5	23	115				97
			19	10	9	
10	21	210				147
			15	15	0	
12	20	240				177
			10	18	-8	
15	18	270				231
			6	20	-14	
20	15	300				331
			2	22	-20	
26	12	312				463
			0	24	-24	
39	8	312				775

b. The profit-maximizing price is either $20 or $21 and the corresponding level of output 12 or 10 units, respectively, since MR = MC (marginal profit is zero) for the eleventh and twelfth units.

c. At a price of $20, TR = $240 and TC = $30 + 177 = $207. Therefore, total profit = TR - TC = $33.

At a price of $21, TR = $210 and TC = $30 + 147 = $177. Total profit = $210 - 177 = $33 also.

2.

a. The completed table follows.

Q	P	TR	MR	MC	Mπ	TVC	AFC
0	$800	$ 0				$ 0	---
			$750	$400	$350		
200	750	150,000				80,000	$300
			650	350	300		
400	700	280,000				150,000	150
			550	300	250		
600	650	390,000				210,000	100
			450	300	150		
800	600	480,000				270,000	75
			350	400	-50		
1,000	550	550,000				350,000	60
			250	500	-250		
1,200	500	600,000				450,000	50
			150	600	-450		
1,400	450	630,000				570,000	42.9

b. The profit-maximizing price and level of output are $600 and 800 chandeliers, respectively. Beyond that point MR < MC, and marginal profit is negative.

3.

a. The completed table appears on the following page.

Q	P	TR	MR	MC	Mπ	TVC	AFC
0	$50	$ 0				$ 0	---
			$45	$20	$25		
100	45	4,500				2,000	$30
			35	15	20		
200	40	8,000				3,500	15
			25	10	15		
300	35	10,500				4,500	10
			15	5	10		
400	30	12,000				5,000	7.5
			5	6	−1		
500	25	12,500				5,600	6.0
			−5	10	−15		
600	20	12,000				6,600	5.0

b. The profit-maximizing price and level of output are $30 and 400 units of output, respectively. Beyond that point, MR < MC.

c. The price elasticity of demand becomes inelastic over the 500 to 600 range of output and $25 to $20 price range, since marginal revenue becomes negative in this range.

Problems on Breakeven Analysis

4.

a.   Breakeven point with the current plant:

$$Q_{BEP} = \frac{TFC}{P - AVC} = \frac{\$1 \text{ million}}{\$20 - 10} = 100,000 \text{ engines.}$$

Breakeven point with the proposed plant:

$$Q_{BEP} = \frac{\$1.8 \text{ million}}{\$15 - 5} = 180,000 \text{ engines.}$$

b.

Profit with the current plant:

TR = 1,000,000 X $20   = $20,000,000

TC = 1,000,000 X $10 + $1,000,000 = 11,000,000

Total Profit   = $ 9,000,000

Profit with the proposed plant:

TR = 1,500,000 X $15   = $22,500,000
TC = 1,500,000 X $5 + $1,800,000 =   9,300,000

Total Profit   = $13,200,000

5.

a.

$$Q_{BEP} = \frac{\$1,200,000}{\$400 - 250} = 8,000 \text{ tons}$$

b.

Profit Before Plant Expansion:
TR = 9,000 X $400 = $3,600,000
TVC = 9,000 X $250 = 2,250,000

TFC   = 1,200,000
Total Profit   = $ 150,000

Profit After Plant Expansion:

TR = 16,000 X $380 = $6,080,000

TVC = 16,000 X 220 = 3,520,000

TFC   = 3,000,000

Total Profit   = $ <440,000>

The firm should not undertake the plant expansion unless it believes that it can sell substantially more than 16,000 tons of steel per year at a price of $380.

6.

a.

Total Variable Cost:

Laundry	$ 44,800
Room Supplies	22,400
Salaries and Wages	89,600
Telephones	4,480
Utilities	33,600
Advertising	11,200
Maintenance	40,320
Miscellaneous	22,400
Total	$268,800

$$\text{Average Variable Cost} = \frac{TVC}{Q} = \frac{\$268,800}{11,200} = \$12.00$$

Total Fixed Cost:

Laundry	$ 4,000
Salaries and Wages	20,000
Telephones	4,000
Utilities	2,000
Advertising	1,000
Office Supplies	6,000
Dues	2,000
Property Taxes, License Fees	81,000
Depreciation	160,000
Insurance	50,000
Interest	230,000
Total	$560,000

The breakeven point number of rooms occupied per month is equal to

$$Q_{BEP} = \frac{\$560,000}{\$80 - 24} = 10,000 \text{ rooms per month.}$$

If all 600 rooms are occupied every day of the month, the total number of rooms that it is possible to have occupied is 600 X 30 = 18,000 rooms. Therefore, the percent occupancy required for the hotel to break even is equal to

$$\frac{10,000}{18,000} \times 100\%, \text{ or approximately } 55.6\%.$$

b.

Casa Rio must look at the difference between the incremental revenue and the incremental cost from this proposal.

Incremental Revenue:

100 Rooms X $40 X 5 days = $20,000

Incremental Cost:

100 Rooms X $24 X 5 days = <u>12,000</u>

Incremental Profit: <u>$ 8,000</u>

c.

In this case, Casa Rio must also take into account the lost profit contribution on the rooms that would have been occupied at the $80 rate.

Increase in profit from part (b) $8,000

Opportunity cost of lost profit
     contribution from the 20
     rooms:

30 Rooms x $56 X 5 days =   <u>8,400</u>

Incremental Profit   <u>$ <400></u>

In this case, Casa Rio should not accept the convention offer.

Profit-Maximization Problems Involving Calculus

7. In order to find the profit-maximizing level of output (number of steers), we first need to determine the MR and MC functions, and set MR - MC = 0.

Since P is constant at $540, MR is also equal to $540.

$$MC = \frac{dTC}{dQ} = 240 - 20Q + Q^2$$

For profit-maximization, MR - MC = 0, or

$$540 - 240 + 20Q - Q^2 = 0.$$

Multiplying the above equation by (-1) and summing terms we get

$$Q^2 - 20Q - 300 = 0.$$

Solving for Q, we factor the expression above and find

$$(Q - 30)(Q + 10) = 0.$$

Thus, Q = 30 at the profit-maximizing point. (The Q = -10 value does not make economic sense.)

Note: The second order condition for a maximum is satisfied at Q = 30, since the value of the second derivative of the total profit function [20 - 2Q] is equal to -40 at that point.

8.

  a. The first step is to derive the total revenue and the total cost functions.

  To derive the total revenue function, we must first get each demand function in the form where P is a function of Q:

$$Q_E = 5,600 - 100P_E,$$

$$-100P_E = Q_E - 5600$$

$$P_E = -.01Q_E + 56$$

$$Q_B = 10,400 - 200P_B$$

$$-200P_B = Q_B - 10,400$$

$$P_B = -.005Q_B + 52$$

$$TR = P_E(Q_E) + P_B(Q_B)$$

$$TR = (-.01Q_E + 56)(Q_E) + (-.005Q_B + 52)(Q_B)$$

$$TR = -.01Q_E^2 + 56Q_E - .005Q_B^2 + 52Q_B$$

Since MC is constant, AVC = MC, and

$$TVC = AVC_E(Q_E) + AVC_B(Q_B) = 6Q_E + 2Q_B.$$

The constraint can be stated as

$$400Q_E + 500Q_B = 3,500,000.$$

The constrained total profit function can be written as

$$Z = -.01Q_E^2 + 56Q_E - .005Q_B^2 + 52Q_B - 6Q_E - 2Q_B$$
$$+ \lambda(3,500,000 - 400Q_E - 500Q_B)$$

$$\delta Z/\delta Q_E = -.02Q_E + 50 - 400\lambda = 0 \qquad (1)$$

$$\delta Z/\delta Q_B = -.01Q_B + 50 - 500\lambda = 0 \qquad (2)$$

$$\delta Z/\delta \lambda = 3,500,000 - 400Q_E - 500Q_B = 0 \qquad (3)$$

Multiplying equation (1) by 5 and equation (2) by -4 and adding the two resulting equations, we obtain

$$-1Q_E + 250 - 2,000 = 0$$

$$\underline{.04Q_B - 200 + 2,000 = 0}$$

$$-.1Q_E + .04Q_B + 50 = 0 \qquad (4)$$

Multiplying equation (4) by 100 and *dividing* equation (3) by 100 we get

$$-10Q_E + 4Q_B = -5,000 \qquad (5)$$

$$-4Q_E - 5Q_B = -35,000 \qquad (6)$$

Finally, multiplying equation (5) by 5 and equation (6) by 4 we find

$-50Q_E + 20Q_B = -25,000$

$-16Q_E - 20Q_B = -140,000$

$-66Q_E \qquad = -165,000$

$Q_E = 2,500 \qquad P_E = -.01(2,500) + 56 = \$31$

Substituting the value for Q_E in equation (6) we get

$-4(2,500) - 5Q_B = -35,000$

$-5Q_B = -25,000$

$Q_B = 5,000 \qquad\qquad P_B = -25 + 52 = \$27$

b. Substituting the above value for Q_B into equation (2) we obtain

$-.01(5,000) + 50 - 500\lambda = 0$

$-50 + 50 - 500\lambda = 0$

$500\lambda = 0$

$\lambda = 0$

In this case, the constraint does not limit the firm. The profit-maximizing level of output for each book would be the same without the constraint on the printing press capacity. In other words, the marginal profit from producing another copy of either book would be zero.

MULTIPLE CHOICE QUESTIONS

1. (c); 2. (a); 3. (b); 4. (b); 5. (c).

Appendix 7: Solutions for Practice Problems

Profit-Maximization Problems

1. The objective is to maximize the total profit contribution, given by

$T\pi C = \$1.20R + .50B$,

where R is the number of dozens of sweet rolls and B is the number of loaves of French bread.

The constraints are as follows:

R	$\leq$	60	Powdered Sugar
2R +	2B $\leq$	250	Flour
1/4R + 1/8B $\leq$		20	Butter

Inserting the slack variables we obtain

$$R \qquad + S_1 = 60 \qquad\qquad (1)$$

$$2R + \quad 2B + S_2 = 250 \qquad (2)$$

$$1/4R + 1/8B + S_3 = 20 \qquad (3)$$

These constraints are graphed in the figure below.

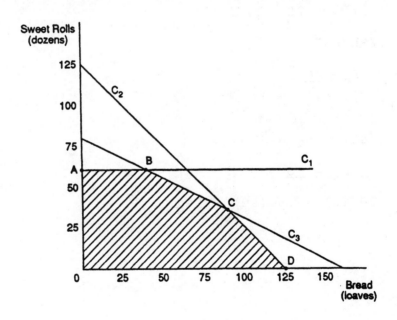

Point A:

B, $S_1 = 0$

From (1),

R = <u>60</u>

From (2),

$$2(60) + 0 + S_2 = 250$$

$$S_2 = \underline{130}$$

From (3),

$$(1/4)(60) + S_3 = 20$$

$$S_3 = \underline{5}$$

$$T\pi C = \$1.20(60) = \underline{\$72}$$

Point B:

$$S_1, S_3 = 0$$

From (1),

$$R = \underline{60}$$

From (3),

$$(1/4)60 + 1/8B = 20$$

$$1/8B = 5$$

$$B = \underline{40}$$

From (2),

$$2(60) + 2(40) + S_2 = 250$$

$$S_2 = \underline{50}$$

$$T\pi C = \$1.20(60) + .50(40) = \underline{\$92}$$

Point C:

$$S_2, S_3 = 0$$

From (2) and (3),

$$2R + \quad 2B = 250 \qquad (4)$$

$$1/4R + 1/8B = \quad 20 \qquad (5)$$

Multiplying equation (5) by -8 and adding the resulting
equation to equation (4) we get

$$2R + 2B = 250$$

$$\underline{-2R - B = -160}$$

$$B = \underline{90}$$

$$2R + 2(90) = 250$$

$$2R = 70$$

$$R = \underline{35}$$

From (1),

$$S_1 = \underline{25}$$

$$T\pi C = \$1.20(35) + .50(90) = \$42 + 45 = \underline{\$87}$$

Point D:

$R, S_2 = 0$

From (2),

$B = \underline{125}$

From (1),

$S_1 = \underline{60}$

From (3),

$$(1/8)(125) + S_3 = 20$$

$$15.625 + S_3 = 20$$

$$S_3 = \underline{4.375}$$

$$T\pi C = \$.50(125) = \underline{\$62.50}$$

Therefore, point B is the optimal point, where R = 60, B = 40, and the total profit contribution is $92. There is an excess quantity of flour available equal to 50 lbs.

2.

a. The objective is to minimize

$$C = 60V_s + 250V_f + 20V_{bu},$$

where V_s is the marginal opportunity cost of the powdered sugar, V_f is the marginal opportunity cost of flour, and V_{bu} is the marginal opportunity cost of butter.

The objective function is subject to the following two constraints:

$$V_s + 2V_f + 1/4V_{bu} \geq 1.20 \qquad \text{Sweet Rolls}$$

$$2V_f + 1/8V_{bu} \geq .50 \qquad \text{French Bread}$$

Placing the slack variables in these constraints we obtain

$$V_s + 2V_f + 1/4V_{bu} - L_R = 1.20 \qquad (1)$$

$$2V_f + 1/8V_{bu} - L_B = .50 \qquad (2)$$

Here, L_R and L_B are the *net* opportunity cost to Barker's of producing rolls and French bread, respectively. Three of the above five variables will have zero values at any possible solution point, and there are 10 possible combinations with this characteristic, as shown below.

Point 1:
_____

V_s , L_R, L_B = 0

From (1) and (2),

$$2V_f + 1/4V_{bu} = 1.20$$
$$\underline{-2V_f - 1/8V_{bu} = -.50}$$
$$1/8V_{bu} = .70$$
$$V_{bu} = \underline{\$5.60}$$

From (2),

$$2V_f + .70 = .50$$
$$2V_f = -.20$$
$$V_f = \underline{\$-.10}$$

Not a feasible solution, $V_f < 0$

Point 2:

V_f, L_R, $L_B = 0$

From (2),

$1/8V_{bu} = .50$

$V_{bu} = \underline{\$4.00}$

From (1),

$V_s + (1/4)(4) = 1.20$

$V_s = \underline{\$.20}$

$C = 60(\$.20) + 20(\$4) = \underline{\$92}$

Point 3

V_{bu}, L_R, $L_B = 0$

From (2),

$2V_f = .50$

$V_f = \underline{\$.25}$

From (1),

$V_s + 2(.25) = 1.20$

$V_s = \underline{\$.70}$

$C = 60(\$.70) + 250(\$.25) = \$42 + 62.50 = \underline{\$104.50}$

Point 4:

V_s, V_f, $L_R = 0$

From (1),

$1/4V_{bu} = 1.20$

$V_{bu} = \underline{\$4.80}$

From (2),

$(1/8)(4.80) - L_B = .50$

$$.60 - L_B = .50$$

$$- L_B = -.10$$

$$L_B = \underline{\$.10}$$

$$C = 20(\$4.80) = \underline{\$96}$$

Point 5:

V_s, V_{bu}, $L_R = 0$

From (1),

$$2V_f = 1.20$$

$$V_f = \underline{\$.60}$$

From (2),

$$2(.60) - L_B = .50$$

$$1.20 - L_B = .50$$

$$L_B = \underline{\$.70}$$

$$C = 250(\$.60) = \underline{\$150}$$

Point 6

V_f, V_{bu}, $L_R = 0$

From (1),

$$V_s = \underline{\$1.20}$$

From (2),

$$-L_B = .50$$

$$L_B = \underline{\$-.50}$$

Not a feasible solution, $L_B < 0$

Point 7:

V_S, V_f, L_B = 0

From (2),

$1/8V_{bu}$ = .50

$\quad$ V_{bu} = $\underline{\$4.00}$

From (1),

$(1/4)(4)$ - L_R = 1.20

$\qquad\qquad$ L_R = $\underline{\$-.20}$

Not a feasible solution, L_R < 0

Point 8:

V_S, V_{bu}, L_B = 0

From (2),

$2V_f$ = .50

$\quad$ V_f = $\underline{\$.25}$

From (1),

$2(.25)$ - L_R = 1.20

$\qquad\qquad$ - L_R = .70

$\qquad\qquad$ L_R = $\underline{\$-.20}$

Not a feasible solution, L_R < 0

Point 9:

V_f, V_{bu}, L_B = 0

Impossible--violates the second constraint

Point 10:

V_S, V_f, V_{bu} = 0

Not a feasible solution since L_R, L_B < 0

Thus, the optimal point is Point 2, where V_f, L_R, and L_B are equal to zero. Actually, the answers to the primary program in problem 1 would tell us that this is the optimal point since both sweet rolls and French bread are produced and there is an excess quantity of flour at the profit-maximizing point in that problem. Note that at this point C = $92, the same value that we found for total profit contribution at the optimal point in problem 1.

b. The marginal opportunity cost of another pound of powdered sugar is $.20, the marginal opportunity cost of another pound of butter is $4.00, the marginal opportunity cost of another pound of flour is zero (there is excess flour available), the net opportunity cost to Barker's of producing rolls and French bread is zero for both products, and the total opportunity cost to the firm of all three resources is $92, the total profit contribution received from producing the optimal quantity of sweet rolls and French bread.

3. The objective is to maximize the total profit contribution, given by

$$T\pi C = \$ \ 6P + 4R,$$

where P is the number of painted pots and R is the number of plain red clay pots.

The constraints are as follows:

$$6P + \ 6R \leq 240 \qquad \text{Oven}$$

$$.4P + .2R \leq \ 12 \qquad \text{Potter's Wheel}$$

$$P \qquad \leq \ 24 \qquad \text{Painter Labor}$$

Inserting the slack variables we obtain

$$6P + \ 6R + S_1 = 240 \qquad (1)$$

$$.4P + .2R + S_2 = \ 12 \qquad (2)$$

$$P \qquad + S_3 = \ 24 \qquad (3)$$

These constraints are graphed in the following figure.

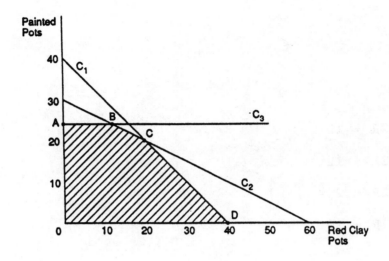

Point A:

R, S_3 = 0

From (3),

P = <u>24</u>

From (1),

6(24) + S_1 = 240

144   + S_1 = 240

       S_1 = <u>96</u>

From (2),

.4(24) + S_2 = 12

  9.6 + S_2 = 12

       S_2 = <u>2.4</u>

TπC = \$6(24) = <u>\$144</u>

Point B:

S_2, S_3 = 0

From (1),

P = 24

From (2),

.4(24) + .2R = 12

9.6 + .2R = 12

.2R = 2.4

R = 12

From (1),

6(24) + 6(12) + S_1 = 240

144 + 72 + S_1 = 240

S_1 = 24

TπC = \$6(24) + 4(12) = \$192

Point C:

S_1, S_2 = 0

From (1) and (2),

6P + 6R = 240   (4)

.4P + .2R = 12   (5)

Dividing equation (4) by -6, multiplying equation (5) by 5, and adding the two equations, we get

- P - R = -40

2P + R = 60

P = 20

Also,

2(20) + R = 60

R = 20

From (3),

$20 + S_3 = 24$

$S_3 = \underline{4}$

$T\pi C = \$6(20) + 4(20) = \underline{\$200}$

Point D:

$P, S_1 = 0$

From (3),

$S_3 = \underline{24}$

From (1),

$6R = 240$

$R = \underline{40}$

From (2),

$.2(40) + S_2 = 12$

$8 + S_2 = 12$

$S_2 = \underline{4}$

$T\pi C = \$4(40) = \underline{\$160}$

Therefore, Point C is the optimal point, where P = 20 painted pots, R = 20 red clay pots, and the total profit contribution is $200. There is an excess quantity of painter labor available equal to 4 hours.

4.

  a. The objective is to minimize

  $C = 240V_O + 12V_w + 24V_{pl}$,

  where V_O is the marginal opportunity cost of oven time, V_w is the marginal opportunity cost of potter's wheel time, and V_{pl} is the marginal opportunity cost of painter labor time. The objective function gives the total opportunity cost values assigned to the fixed inputs.

The objective function is subject to the following two constraints:

$$6V_O + .4V_W + V_{pl} \geq 6 \qquad \text{Painted Pots}$$
$$6V_O + .2V_W \qquad \geq 4 \qquad \text{Red Clay Pots}$$

The constraints state that the sum of the opportunity cost values placed on each fixed input multiplied by the quantities required of each respective input must be greater than or equal to the profit contribution for one pot. The top constraint applies to painted pots, whereas the bottom constraint applies to red clay pots.

Placing the slack variables in these constraints we obtain

$$6V_O + .4V_W + V_{pl} - L_P = 6 \qquad (1)$$
$$6V_O + .2V_W \qquad - L_R = 4 \qquad (2)$$

Here L_P and L_R are the net opportunity cost to Pat's of producing painted pots and red clay pots, respectively.

b. As we saw in problem (2), three of the above five variables will have zero values at any possible solution point, and there are 10 possible combinations with this characteristic. However, we know from the solution in problem (3) that the optimal point will occur where L_P and L_R are both equal to zero, since Pat's will produce both types of pots to maximize the total profit contribution. Moreover, V_{pl} will be zero since there is excess painter labor time available at the optimal point.

Where V_{pl}, L_P, and $L_R = 0$:
_____

$$6V_O + .4V_W = 6$$

$$6V_O + .2V_W = 4$$

Multiplying the second equation above by -1 and adding the two equations we get

$$6V_O + .4V_W = 6$$

$$-6V_O - .2V_W = -4$$

$$.2V_W = 2$$

$$V_W = \$\underline{10}$$

Also,

$$6V_O + .2(10) = 4$$

$$6V_O + 2 = 4$$

$$6V_O = 2$$

$$V_O = \underline{\$1/3 \text{ or about } \$.333}$$

$$C = 240(\$1/3) + 12(\$10) + 24(0) = \underline{\$200}$$

Cost-Minimization Problem

5.

a. The objective is to minimize the total cost of leasing, given by

TC = \$20,000M + 15,000D,

where M is the number of mall stores and D is the number of downtown stores.

The constraints are as follows:

$6,000M + 8,000D \geq 120,000$	Walk Past
$800M + 400D \geq 9,600$	Income
$4,000M + 4,000D \geq 72,000$	Television

Inserting the slack variables we obtain

$$6,000M + 8,000D - S_1 = 120,000 \qquad (1)$$

$$800M + 400D - S_2 = 9,600 \qquad (2)$$

$$4,000M + 4,000D - S_3 = 72,000 \qquad (3)$$

These constraints are graphed in the figure below.

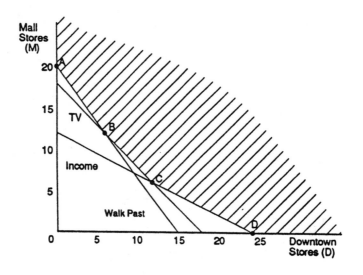

Point A:

$D, S_1 = 0$

From (1),

$6,000M = 120,000$

$M = \underline{20}$

From (2),

$800(20) - S_2 = 9,600$

$16,000 - S_2 = 9,600$

$S_2 = \underline{6,400}$

From (3),

$4,000(20) - S_3 = 72,000$

$80,000 - S_3 = 72,000$

$S_3 = \underline{8,000}$

TC = $20,000(20) = $\underline{\$400,000}$

<u>Point B:</u>

S_1, $S_3 = 0$

From (1) and (3),

$$6,000M + 8,000D = 120,000 \qquad (4)$$

$$4,000M + 4,000D = 72,000 \qquad (5)$$

Multiplying equation (5) by -2 and adding the resulting two equations we obtain

$$6,000M + 8,000D = 120,000$$

$$\underline{-8,000M - 8,000D = -144,000}$$

$$-2,000M = -24,000$$

$$M = \underline{12}$$

Also,

$$4,000(12) + 4,000D = 72,000$$

$$48,000 + 4,000D = 72,000$$

$$4,000D = 24,000$$

$$D = \underline{6}$$

From (2),

$$800(12) + 400(6) - S_2 = 9,600$$

$$9,600 + 2,400 - S_2 = 9,600$$

$$S_2 = \underline{2,400}$$

TC = $20,000(12) + 15,000(6) = $240,000 + 90,000 = $\underline{\$330,000}$

<u>Point C:</u>

S_2, $S_3 = 0$

From (2) and (3),

$$800M + \quad 400D = \quad 9,600 \qquad (6)$$

$$4,000M + 4,000D = 72,000 \qquad (7)$$

Multiplying (6) by -10 and adding the resulting two equations, we get

$$-8,000M - 4,000D = -96,000$$

$$\underline{\ 4,000M + 4,000D = \quad 72,000\ }$$

$$-4,000M \qquad\qquad = -24,000$$

$$M = \underline{6}$$

From (7),

$$4,000(6) + 4,000D = 72,000$$

$$24,000 + 4,000D = 72,000$$

$$4,000D = 48,000$$

$$D = \underline{12}$$

From (1),

$$6,000(6) + 8,000(12) - S_1 = 120,000$$

$$36,000 + \quad 96,000 \ - S_1 = 120,000$$

$$132,000 \ - S_1 = 120,000$$

$$S_1 = \underline{\ 12,000\ }$$

$$TC = \$20,000(6) + 15,000(12) = \$120,000 + 180,000 = \underline{\$300,000}$$

Point D:

$M, S_2 = 0$

From (2),

$$400D = 9,600$$

$$D = \underline{24}$$

From (1),

$8,000(24) - S_1 = 120,000$

$\qquad 192,000 - S_1 = 120,000$

$\qquad\qquad S_1 = \underline{72,000}$

From (3),

$4,000(24) - S_3 = 72,000$

$\qquad 96,000 - S_3 = 72,000$

$\qquad\qquad S_3 = \underline{24,000}$

$TC = \$15,000(24) = \underline{\$360,000}$

Therefore, the optimal point is at Point C, where the number of mall stores is 6 and the number of downtown stores is 12.

b. The total cost to the firm of leasing these stores is $300,000.

c. The dual program objective is to maximize

$V = 120,000V_1 + 9,600V_2 + 72,000V_3,$

where V is an imputed value or cost to the firm of the three constraints in the primal program. It is obtained by finding an imputed value that is really the marginal cost to the firm of changing each individual constraint. V_1 is the marginal cost of the "walk past" constraint, V_2 is the marginal cost of the income constraint, and V_3 is the marginal cost of the television constraint.

The objective function is subject to the following two constraints:

$6,000V_1 + 800V_2 + 4,000V_3 \leq 20,000$ Mall Stores

$8,000V_1 + 400V_2 + 4,000V_3 \leq 15,000$ Downtown Stores

Inserting the slack variables we obtain

$6,000V_1 + 800V_2 + 4,000V_3 + L_M = 20,000$ (1)

$$8,000V_1 + 400V_2 + 4,000V_3 + L_D = 15,000 \qquad (2)$$

The two variables L_M and L_D represent the net opportunity cos tor relative inefficiency of using mall stores and downtown stores, respectively. If neither store is relatively inefficient, L_M and L_D will be zero, and the firm will lease both types of stores.

From our answer in part (a), we know that at the optimal point, LM and L_D are equal to zero. Also V_1 is equal to zero, since the "walk past" constraint in the primal program is more than met at this point.

Thus, from (1) and (2),

$$800V_2 + 4,000V_3 = 20,000$$
$$400V_2 + 4,000V_3 = 15,000$$

Subtracting the second equation from the first, we get

$$400V_2 = 5,000$$
$$V_2 = \underline{\$12.50}$$

Also,

$$400(12.50) + 4,000V_3 = 15,000$$
$$5,000 + 4,000V_3 = 15,000$$
$$4,000V_3 = 10,000$$
$$V_3 = \underline{\$2.50}$$

$V = 0 + 9,600(\$12.50) + 72,000(\$2.50) = \$180,000 + 120,000 = \$300,000$, the same value as we found for the primal objective function at the optimal point in part (a), above. The marginal cost of increasing the income constraint is thus $12.50 per month, whereas the marginal cost of increasing the television constraint is $2.50.

CHAPTER 8:   Solutions for Practice Problems

Diagrams of Perfect Competition and Monopoly

1.

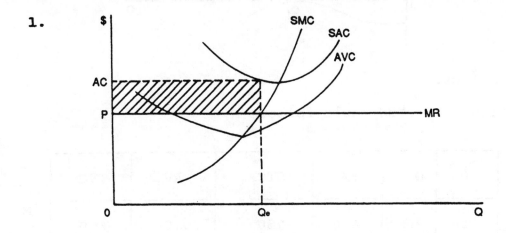

2.

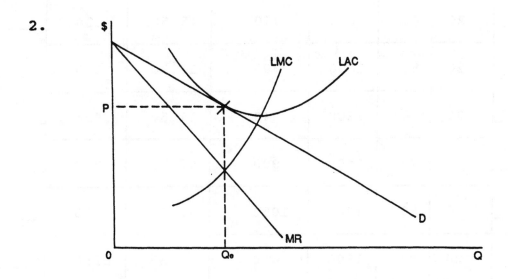

3.

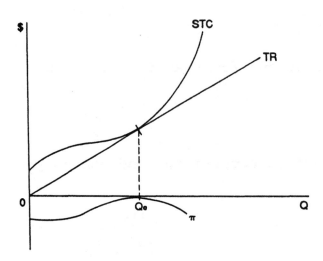

Tabular Problems.

4.   The completed table follows.

	P	Q	TR	STC	AVC	TVC	
MR							MC
	20	30	600	750	20.00	600	
20							2
	20	40	800	770	15.50	620	
20							3
	20	50	1000	800	13.00	650	
20							4
	20	60	1200	840	11.50	690	
20							6
	20	70	1400	900	10.71	750	
20							15
	20	80	1600	1050	11.25	900	
20							39
	20	90	1800	1440	14.33	1290	

a.   Perfect competition, since the price is constant for all of
     the above levels of output.

b.   The closest the firm can come to meeting the condition that
     MR = MC without MR < MC is at 80 units of output.   Total
     profit is equal to TR - STC = $1,600 - 1,050 = $550.

c.   No, because economic profit cannot exist in the long run for
     a perfectly competitive firm.

5.   The completed table follows.

P	Q	TR	MR	TC	MC
10	20	200		100	
			8		6
9	40	360		220	
			6		4
8	60	480		300	
			4		7
7	80	560		440	
			2		11
6	100	600			16
			0	660	
5	120	600		980	

a.   Because a perfectly competitive firm can sell as large
     a quantity of output as it wishes at the going market
     price.   In the table above, the firm must lower price
     in order to sell a larger quantity.

b.   P = $8, and Q = 60

     The profit-maximizing condition is that MR = MC, or as
     close as the firm can come to meeting this condition as
     long as MR is not less than MC.

c.   Total profit is equal to TR - TC = $480 - 300 = $180.

     Yes.   At any other price TR - TC will be less than at a
     price of $8.

Profit Maximization Using Equations

6.

    a.   The profit-maximizing quantity will be where MR = MC, or

$$48 - .1Q = 4 + .12Q$$

$$- .22Q = - 44$$
$$Q = \underline{200}$$

$$P = - .05Q + 48$$
$$= - .05(200) + 48$$
$$= - 10 + 48$$
$$= \underline{\$38}$$

    b.   TR = P X Q = \$38 X 200 = \$7,600

$$TC = 3,000 + 4(200) + (.06)(200)^2$$
$$= 3,000 + 800 + (.06)(40,000)$$
$$= 3,800 + 2,400$$
$$= \$6,200$$

Total profit = \$7,600 - 6,200 = $\underline{\$1,400}$.

7.

    a.   Profit will be maximized where P = MR = MC:

$$40 = 20 + .04Q$$
$$.04Q = 20$$
$$Q = \underline{500}$$

    b.   No. The firm can sell as many units as it wishes at the going market price. However, it will sell <u>no</u> units at a higher price.

8.

a. The first step is to find the SMC and MR functions.

$$SMC = dSTC/dQ = 90 - 20Q + Q^2$$

$$Q = 58 - 0.2P$$

$$- .2P = Q - 58$$

$$P = - 5Q + 290$$

$$TR = P \times Q = - 5Q^2 + 290Q$$

$$MR = dTR/dQ = - 10Q + 290$$

Setting MR = SMC we find:

$$- 10Q + 290 = 90 - 20Q + Q^2$$

$$Q^2 - 10Q - 200 = 0$$

$$(Q + 10)(Q - 20) = 0$$

$$Q + 10 = 0 \qquad\qquad\qquad Q - 20 = 0$$

Q = -10 Not economically   Q = <u>20</u>
        reasonable.

b. $P = - 5Q + 290$

$$= - 5(20) + 290$$

$$= - 100 + 290$$

$$= \underline{\$190}$$

c.

$$TR = P \times Q = \$190 \times 20 = \$3,800$$

$$STC = 700 + (90)(20) - (10)(20)^2 + (1/3)(20)^{.3}$$

$$= 700 + 1,800 - 10(400) + (1/3)(8,000)$$

$$= 700 + 1,800 - 4,000 + 2,666.67$$

$$= \$1,166.67$$

$$Total\ profit = TR - STC = \$3,800 - 1,166.67$$

$$= \$2,633.33$$

9.

a. $STC = 10,500 + 290(100) - 2(100)^2 + .01(100)^3$

$= 10,500 + 29,000 - 2(10,000) + .01(1,000,000)$

$= 10,500 + 29,000 - 20,000 + 10,000 = \$29,500$

$SAC = STC/Q = \$29,500/100 = \underline{\$295}$.

b. $SMC = dSTC/dQ = 290 - 4Q + .03Q^2$

Profit will be maximized where P = MR = SMC:

$190 = 290 - 4Q + .03Q^2$

$.03Q^2 - 4Q + 100 = 0$

$(3Q - 100)(.01Q - 1) = 0$

$3Q - 100 = 0$ $.01Q - 1 = 0$

     $3Q = 100$ $.01Q = 1$

       $Q = 33.33$ $Q = 100$

There are two values for Q that satisfy the first order condition that MR - MC = 0. We shall now check the second order condition for each value.

The total profit function = TR - TC

$= 190Q - 10,500 - 290Q + 2Q^2 - .01Q3$

$dT\pi/dQ = 190 - 290 + 4Q - .03Q^2$

$= -100 + 4Q - .03Q^2$

$d^2T\pi/dQ^2 = 4 - .06Q$

At Q = 33.33,

$d^2T\pi/dQ^2 = 4 - .06(33.33) = 4 - 2 = 2 > 0$, so this is a minimum point

At Q = 100,

$d^2T\pi/dQ^2 = 4 - .06(100) = 4 - 6 = - 2 < 0$, <u>so this point is a maximum point</u>.

Thus, the profit-maximizing level of output is <u>100 units</u>.

$$TR = \$190 \times 100 = \$19,000$$

STC = \$29,500 [from part (a)]

Total profit = TR - STC = \$19,000 - 29,500 = <u>- \$10,500.</u>

The firm is incurring an economic loss of \$10,500.

c.   Long-run industry equilibrium will occur when each firm is producing where P = minimum LAC.

$$LAC = LTC/Q = 425 - 1.5Q + .002Q^2$$

LAC will be at a minimum where dLAC/dQ = 0 (the second order condition is met at that point):

$$dLAC/dQ = -1.5 + .004Q = 0$$

$$.004Q = 1.5$$

$$Q = \underline{375}$$

At Q = 375:

$$LAC = 425 - (1.5)(375) + .002(375)^2$$

$$= 425 - 562.50 + .002(140,625)$$

$$= 425 - 562.50 + 281.25$$

$$= \underline{\$143.75}.$$

Since P = LAC at this point, total (economic) profit will be zero.

MULTIPLE CHOICE QUESTIONS

   1. (**a**);   2. (**d**);   3. (**a**);   4. (**a**);   5. (**d**).

CHAPTER 9: Solutions for Practice Problems

1.   **Problem on Monopolistic Competition**

The appropriate diagram appears on the following page.

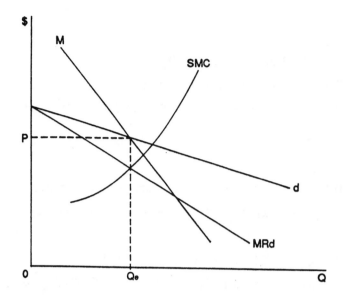

In the figure given on p. 137, the firm does not have enough market share to sell Q_e. It has not estimated d correctly and must find a new d that yields MR_d = MC at the intersection of d and M, as above.

2. The Duopoly Case

(i)

The revenues of the two clubs will be maximized where the market marginal revenue is equal to zero. The market marginal revenue curve is derived as follows from the demand curve.

$$Q = 3200 - 400P$$
$$-400P = Q - 3200$$
$$P = -.0025Q + 8$$
$$TR = P \times Q = -.0025Q^2 + 8Q$$
$$MR = dTR/dQ = -.005Q + 8$$

Setting marginal revenue equal to zero, we find:

$$MR = -.005Q + 8 = 0$$
$$-.005Q = -8$$
$$\underline{\underline{Q = 1,600 \text{ vehicles parked.}}}$$

The corresponding price is found by substituting for Q in the equation for price:

$$P = -.0025Q + 8 = -.0025(1,600) + 8 = \underline{\$4.00}.$$

(ii)

They will each supply 1/3 of the total quantity demanded at a zero price. The quantity corresponding to a zero price is where

$$P = -.0025Q + 8 = 0$$
$$-.0025Q = -8$$
$$Q = 3,200.$$

The total quantity that the two clubs will supply will be equal to (2/3) of 3,200 = 2,133.33 or approximately 2,133. The corresponding price is found as

$$P = -.0025(2133) + 8 = -5.33 + 8 = \underline{\$2.67}.$$

(iii)

$$\text{Monopolist:} \quad TR = 1,600 \times \$4 = \underline{\$6,400}.$$

$$\text{Cournot:} \quad TR = 2,133 \times \$2.67 = \underline{\$5,695.11}.$$

Price Leadership by a Dominant Firm

3.

a. $Q_L = Q_d - Q_s = 8,520 - 110P - 20 - 15P = 8,500 - 125P$

b. The dominant firm will maximize profit where $MR_L = MC_L$, or

$$68 - .016Q_L = 3.2 + .002Q_L$$
$$-.018Q_L = -64.8$$
$$Q_L = \underline{3,600}.$$

From the demand curve for the dominant firm,

$$P_L = -.008Q_L + 68$$
$$P_L = -.008(3,600) + 68 = -28.80 + 68 = \underline{\$39.20}.$$

c.

$$Q_S = 20 + 15(39.20) = 20 + 588 = \underline{608}.$$
$$Q_d = Q_S + Q_L = 608 + 3,600 = \underline{4,208}.$$

d.

$$TR_L = 3,600 \times \$39.20 = \$141,120$$
$$TC_L = 100,000 + 3.2(3,600) + .001(3,600)^2$$
$$= 100,000 + 11,520 + .001(12,960,000)$$
$$= 100,000 + 11,520 + 12,960$$
$$= \$124,480.$$
$$TR_L - TC_L = \$141,120 - 124,480 = \underline{\$16,640}.$$

4.

a. The first step is to develop the demand and marginal revenue functions for the dominant firm.

$$Q_L = Q_d - Q_S = 5,000 - P - 500 - 3P, \text{ or}$$
$$Q_L = 4,500 - 4P$$

To get the marginal revenue function, we must first solve for P in terms of Q_L:

$$-4P = Q_L - 4,500$$
$$P = -.25Q_L + 1,125$$
$$TR_L = P \times Q_L = -.25Q_L^2 + 1,125Q_L$$
$$MR_L = dTR_L/dQ_L = -.5Q_L + 1,125$$

The marginal cost curve for the dominant firm is

$$MC_L = dTC_L/dQ_L = 5 + 1.5Q_L$$

The profit-maximizing price for the dominant firm will be found where $MR_L = MC_L$:

$$-.5Q_L + 1,125 = 5 + 1.5Q_L$$
$$-2Q_L = -1,120$$
$$Q_L = \underline{560}.$$
$$P = -.25Q_L + 1,125 = -140 + 1,125 = \underline{\$985}.$$

b. From part (a), the quantity supplied by the large firm is equal to <u>560 widgets</u>.

c. Q_S = 500 + 3P = 500 + 3(985) = 500 + 2,955

= 3,455.

d. Q_d = 5,000 - P = Qs + Q_L = 3,455 + 560 = 4,015.

5. **Kinked Demand Curve Oligopoly**

a. The current price will be the one that equates
the quantities from the two demand functions. Setting
Q_1 = Q_2, we obtain:

2,100 - 100P = 3,300 - 200P

100P = 1,200

P = $12.00.

The corresponding quantity sold can be found from either
demand function:

Q = 2,100 - 100P = 2,100-1,200 = 900 square yards

= 3,300 - 200P.

b. The current price is not consistent with profit
maximization.

At Q = 900:

MR_1 = 21 - .02Q_1 = 21 - .02(900) = 21 - 18 = $3

MR_2 = 16.5 - .01Q_2 = 16.5 - .01(900) = 16.5 - 9 = $7.50

MC = 0.75 + .01Q = 0.75 + .01(900) = 0.75 + 9 = $9.75

Since MC is greater than the higher MR, Canauba is not
producing at the profit-maximizing level of output.

c. Canauba Carpet would maximize profit by selling 900 square
yards of carpet at a price of $12.00 per square yard as long
as its marginal cost was in the $3 to $7.50 range at that
level of output.

6.

a. Again, we must find the price that equates the quantities from the two demand functions. Setting $Q_1 = Q_2$, we obtain:

440 - 4P = 250 - 2P

  - 2P = - 190

    P = $95.

Substituting for price in either demand function we find

Q = 440 - 4(95) = 440 - 380 = 60 = 250 - 2(95).

b. We must now find the marginal revenue functions corresponding to each demand curve. First, we must solve each demand function for price, then multiply this equation by Q to derive the corresponding total revenue function, and then find the MR function.

Q_1 = 440 - 4P

-4P = Q_1 - 440

  P = - .25Q_1 + 110

TR1 = - .25Q_1^2 + 110Q_1

MR_1 = dTR_1/dQ_1 = - .50Q_1 + 110

  Q_2 = 250 - 2P

-2P = Q_2 - 250

  P = - .5Q_2 + 125

TR_2 = - .5Q_2^2 + 125Q_2

MR_2 = $dTR_2/dQ2$ = - Q_2 + 125

SMC = dSTC/dQ = 20 - .2Q + .012Q^2

At Q = 60:

  MC = 20 -.2(60) + .012(60) = 20 - 12 + 43.2 = $51.20

MR_1 = - .50(60) + 110 = - 30 + 110 = $80

MR_2 = - 60 + 125 = $65

Since MC is less than the lower MR at Q = 60, NCA is not maximizing its profit at this point.

c. Now,

$MC = 20 - .2Q + .018Q^2$

At $Q = 60$,

$MC = 20 - 12 + 64.8 = \$72.80$

With the new marginal cost function, NCA's profit-maximizing price and quantity are $95 and 60 units of output, respectively.

7. Operation of a Multiple-Plant Firm

You and Jim will maximize profit by producing where

$MC_a = MC_b = MC_c = 150$

For the first mine: $MC_a = 10 + .008Q_a = 150$; $.008Q_a = 140$, and $Q_a = 17,500$.

For the second mine: $MC_b = 40 + .002Q_b = 150$; $.002Q_b = 110$ and $Q_b = 55,000$.

For the third mine: $MC_c = 6 + .015Q_c = 150$; $.015Q_c = 144$ and $Q_c = 9,600$.

The total quantity supplied will be $Q_a + Q_b + Q_c = 17,500 + 55,000 + 9,600 = 82,100$.

$TR = P \times Q = \$150 \times 82,100 = \$12,315,000$

$TC = \$2,000,000 + AVC_a \times Q_a + AVC_b \times Q_b + AVC_c \times Q_c$

$= \$2,000,000 + 1,400,000 + 5,225,000 + 748,800$

$= \$9,373,800$

Total Profit $= TR - TC = \$12,315,000 - 9,373,800$

$= \underline{\$2,941,200}$.

MULTIPLE CHOICE QUESTIONS

1. (**a**); 2. (**d**); 3. (**a**); 4. (**d**); 5. (**d**).

CHAPTER 10:   Solutions for Practice Problems

Game Theory

1.

| | Pizza Palace | |
	Don't Accept Coupons	Accept Coupons
Mamma Mia's Don't Accept Coupons	40^M 60	35 90^P
Accept Coupons	30 70	45^M 80^P

In the preceding payoff matrix, the **M** superscripts indicate Mamma Mia's strategic choices, while the **P** superscripts indicate those of Pizza Palace.

  a.   Mamma Mia's does not have a dominant strategy. Mamma Mia's will not accept coupons if Pizza Palace doesn't but will accept them if Pizza Palace does.

  b.   Pizza Palace does have a dominant strategy, since it is best off to accept coupons regardless of what strategy Mamma's chooses.

  c.   Both will accept coupons. There is a Nash equilibrium in the lower right-hand cell. Since the dominant strategy for Pizza Palace is to accept, Mamma Mia's best strategy is to also accept coupons.

2.   In the following payoff matrix, the strategic choices of AA are marked with an **A** superscript, while those of UA have a **U** superscript.

| | UA | |
	Fare Special	Double Miles
AA Fare Special	2.5^A 2.0^U	3.0^A 1.8
Double Miles	2.0 1.8	2.7 2.1^U

a. As the superscripts show, AA has a dominant strategy, since it will offer the fare special no matter what UA does.

b. There is a Nash equilibrium in the upper left-hand cell, so both airlines will offer the fare special.

3. In the following payoff matrix, the strategic choices of Ralphson's are marked with an **R** superscript, while those of Safeger's have an **S** superscript.

Safeger's

	Keep Cards	Eliminate Cards
Keep Cards Ralphson's	130^R 105^S	112 90
Eliminate Cards	90 110	120^R 130^S

a. As the superscripts show, neither firm has a dominant strategy. If one firm keeps discount cards, so will the other. If one firm eliminates cards, so will the other.

b. The game has two Nash equilibria, upper left-hand cell and lower right-hand cell. However, we cannot say which will be the result, since Ralphson's is better off if both firms keep the cards but Safeger's is best off if both eliminate them.

c. Yes, Ralphson's will choose to keep the cards, since that is its best option of the two Nash equilibria. Safeger's will follow suit, and its payoff will be 105.

d. Yes, there is a first-mover advantage in the game. Note that if Safeger's moves first, cards will be eliminated, and it will obtain a 130 payoff instead of 105. In this instance, Ralphson's payoff is 120.

4. a. Yes, East-West is best off to choose to obtain wide-body aircraft no matter what Trans Nation does, so EW does have a dominant strategy.

b. By backwards induction, both firms will choose to switch to wide-body planes. We have already noted that this is a dominant strategy for EW. That ensures an outcome on the upper branch from each EW decision node. Given this, Trans Nation has the best result by going to the uppermost branch, where its payoff is 22 and EW gets 15.

Incentives and Contracting

5. a. For the given demand curve, Q = 30,000 - 5,000P, the price equation is P = 6 - .0002Q. The $0.90 AVC of the spuds is their MC, and MR = 6 - .0004Q. Thus

$$6 - .0004Q = 0.90; \quad Q = 5.1/.0004 = \underline{12,750}$$

$$P = 6 - .0002(12,750) = \underline{\$3.45}$$

This price is much greater than AVC, so you should operate.

b. Ahha! The franchisor is a sharpie. He knows that revenue will be maximized where MR = 0, not where MR = 0.90. This will occur when Q = 15,000, which requires that P = $3. That solution will yield the franchisor .2(15,000)(3) = $9,000 royalty. If you calculate the royalty on the TR that would be generated at Q = 12,750 and P = $3.45, you will find it is less. The contract, therefore, has a built-in conflict between you and the franchisor.

6. a. To answer this part, construct the following table. Remember that only 20 percent of jokes will be used on the show and generate commission. (We round jokes used to the nearest whole number to calculate commission. Marginal cost and marginal benefit are in dollars per hour.)

Hours Worked	Total Jokes Produced	Total Commission	Marginal Benefit ($)	Marginal Cost ($)
20	20	$ 800		
			40	30
30	30	1,200		
			40	35
40	38	1,600		
			20	50
50	44	1,800		
			20	60
60	48	2,000		

You will work 40 hours and produce 38 jokes. The opportunity cost of an hour of your time is $50 beyond 40 hours worked, but with your limited ability to produce more jokes per hour, your commission only amounts to $20 per hour.

b.   Offer something more than $500 for the ninth joke used and something over $600 for the tenth. These commission increases would more than cover the marginal opportunity cost of your time.

MULTIPLE CHOICE QUESTIONS

1. **(d)**;   2. **(c)**;   3. **(b)**;   4. **(a)**;   5. **(d)**

CHAPTER 11: Solutions for Practice Problems

Problem on Markup Pricing

1. As discussed in the chapter, the relationship between elasticity and the profit-maximizing markup on a constant AVC is

   dollar amount of markup = $AVC[-1/(e_p + 1)]$.

   In this problem, AVC is the manufacturer's cost multiplied by 1.2, plus $4.00 per drum handling. This comes to $140(1.2) + $4 = $172. Thus,

   dollar amount of markup = $172[-1/(-3.5 + 1)]$

$$= \$172(0.4) = \underline{\$68.80}.$$

   The surfacer should be sold for $172 + 68.80 = $240.80 per drum.

Problems on Joint Products

2. a.   The isorevenue line will be tangent where A = 10 and B = 8.

   b.   It will shift outward (to the right), since the same budget will produce higher levels of output.

3. a.   Solving the problem for $(MR_m + MR_t)$ = MC will yield an answer of Q = 23,000. However, $MR_t < 0$ at any quantity

greater than 20,000. Therefore, the correct answer is obtained by letting MR_m = MC as follows:

$$31 - 0.001Q = 1 + 0.0002Q; \quad Q = 25,000.$$

This will be the quantity produced.

b. AAC should sell all 25,000 of the muffs but should sell only 20,000 tails since MR_t < 0 beyond 20,000.

c. $P_m = 31 - 0.0005Q_m = 31 - 12.50 = \$18.50$.

$P_t = 16 - 0.0004Q_t = 16 - 8 = \$8.00$.

d. TR = 25,000(18.5) + 20,000(8) = 622,500

TC = 25,000(16) = 400,000; Profit = \$222,500.

4. a. Solving this problem for $(MR_v + MR_c)$ = MC yields an answer of Q = 27,000. However, MR_c < 0 for any quantity greater than 25,000. Therefore, the correct answer occurs where MR_v = MC , or

$$64 - 0.0016Q = 2 + 0.0004Q; \quad Q = 31,000.$$

b. KC should sell all 31,000 tons of the vermiculite but only 25,000 tons of potter's clay, the latter to avoid the range where MR_c < 0.

c. $P_v = 64 - 0.0008Q_v = 64 - 24.8 = \$39.20$.

$P_c = 100 - 0.0002Q_c = 100 - 50 = \$50.00$.

d. TR = 31,000(39.20) + 25,000(50) = 2,465,200

TC = 1,500,000 + 2(31,000) + 0.0002(31,000)^2 = 1,754,200; Profit = \$711,000.

Transfer Product Problem

5. a. Freeway will determine the number of audio units to sell where net marginal revenue from their sales is equal to the price of the transfer product, or

$Q_a = 10,000 - 50P_a; \quad P_a = 200 - 0.02Qa;$
$MR_a = 200 - 0.04Q_a,$ and $NMR_a = MR_a - MC_a = 195 - 0.061Q_a.$

Where $NMR_a = P_c,$ $195 - 0.061Q_a = 12; \quad Q_a = 3,000.$

b. P_a = 200 - 0.02Q_a = 200 - 60 = $\underline{\$140}$.

c.   Solution is at MC_c = 12, where 12 is P_c and MR_c.

$0.10 + 0.001Q_c = 12$; $Q_c = \underline{11,900}$.

d.   Coastal should make 11,900 - 3,000 = 8,900 units for other producers, since Freeway will buy only 3,000 and additional profit can be made on the balance.

Two-Part Pricing Problem

6.   The fitness center should set its marginal cost of $5 equal to the price equation for its demand curve to obtain the optimal quantity.   Thus, 5 = 7 - 0.2Q, and Q = 2/0.2 = $\underline{10}$. P = 7 - 0.2(10) = $\underline{5}$.   The access fee is obtained by taking 0.5bh for the area of the consumer surplus triangle, or 0.5(10)(7-5) = $\underline{10}$.

Bundling Problem

7.
	Snack Pack	Movie
Male	$3.00	$2.75
Female	$1.80	$3.80

Without bundling, the firm would have to price the snack pack at $1.80 and the movie at $2.75 to get both males and females to purchase both items.   Revenue from one male and one female would be ($1.80 + $2.75)(2) = $9.10.   The upper limit for bundling is the amount the female will pay, or ($1.80 + $3.80) = $5.60, which is less than the male limit of $5.75.   Two of these bundles yield revenue of $11.60, so the gain from bundling is $11.20 - $9.10 = $\underline{\$2.10}$ for one male and one female customer.   The firm should bundle.

Price Discrimination Problem

8.   a.   Solve for the two quantities by setting each market's MR equal to the firm's MC.

$MR_{us} = 15,000 - 10Q_{us} = 800$; $Q_{us} = \underline{1,420}$.

$P_{us} = 15,000 - 5Q_{us} = 15,000 - 7,100 = \underline{\$7,900}$.

$MR_f = 12,500 - 5Q_f = 800$; $Q_f = \underline{2,340}$.

$$P_f = 12{,}500 - 2.5Q_f = 12{,}500 - 5{,}850 = \$6{,}650.$$

b.   TR $= 1{,}420(7{,}900) + 2{,}340(6{,}650) = 26{,}779{,}000;$

TC $= 200{,}000 + 800(3{,}760) = 3{,}208{,}000;$

Profit $= \$23{,}571{,}000.$ Buy stock in this company!

MULTIPLE CHOICE QUESTIONS

1. (b);   2. (b);   3. (d);   4. (b).

CHAPTER 12:   Solutions for Practice Problems

Problems on the Profit-Maximizing Employment of One Variable Input

1. a. The completed table appears on the next page.

    b. The profit-maximizing quantity of labor is 70, the corresponding price is \$1,120, and the quantity of mixers is 8,800. At this point Builder's Equipment comes the closest it can to fulfilling the condition that $MRP_L = MC_L$, without $MRP_L < MC_L$.

    c.
    $$MC = \frac{MC_L}{MP_L} + CC$$

    $$= \frac{15{,}000}{80} + 100$$

    $$= 187.50 + 100 = \underline{\$287.50}$$

    (See next page for solution to Part **a**.)

(Table for Part **a**, Problem 1)

Q of Labor	Q of Mixers	Price of one Mixer	Total Revenue	Arc MR	Arc Net Marg. Rev.	Arc MP_L	Arc MRP_L
0	0	$2,000	$ 0				
				$1,920	$1,820	80	$145,600
10	800	1,920	1,536,000				
				1,720	1,620	120	194,400
20	2,000	1,800	3,600,000				
				1,450	1,350	150	202,500
30	3,500	1,650	5,775,000				
				1,100	1,000	200	200,000
40	5,500	1,450	7,975,000				
				750	650	150	97,500
50	7,000	1,300	9,100,000				
				500	400	100	40,500
60	8,000	1,200	9,600,000				
				320	220	80	17,600
70	8,800	1,120	9,856,000				
				190	90	50	4,500
80	9,300	1,070	9,951,000				
				120	20	20	400
90	9,500	1,050	9,975,000				

2.

  a. The completed table follows.

Quantity of Labor	Quantity of Computers	Price	Total Revenue	Arc MR	Arc NMR_L	Arc MP_L	Arc MRP_L	Arc MC of Output
0	0	$2,800	$ 0					
				$2,600	$2,600	10	$22,000	$ 660
5	50	2,600	130,000					
				2,200	1,800	5	9,000	920
15	100	2,400	240,000					
				1,800	1,400	2	2,800	1,700
40	150	2,200	330,000					
				1,400	1,000	2	2,000	1,700
65	200	2,200	400,000					
				1,000	600	1.25	750	2,480
105	250	1,800	450,000					

  b. The profit-maximizing quantity of labor is 40, the corresponding number of computers is 150, and the price is $2,200. This point is as close as Alamo Instruments can come to where $MRP_L = MC_L$, without $MRP_L < MRP_L$. It is also as close as Alamo Instruments can come to the point where MR = MC, without MR < MC.

3.

  a. The completed table follows.

Quantity of Output	Quantity of Labor	Price of one Pair Glasses	Total Revenue	Arc MR	Arc Net MR	Arc MP_L	Arc MRP_L
0	0	$20	$ 0				
				$18	$17	10	$170
100	10	18	1,800				
				14	13	20	260
200	15	16	3,200				
				10	9	10	90
300	25	14	4,200				
				6	5	5	25
400	45	12	4,800				
				3	2	4.17	8.34
450	57	11	4,950				
				1	0	1	0
500	107	10	5,000				
				-1	-2	0.5	-1
550	207	9	4,950				

  b. The profit-maximizing quantity of sunglasses is 450 pairs,
      the corresponding price is $11, and the quantity of labor is
      57. This is as close as the firm can come to the point where
      $MRP_L = MC_L$ without $MRP_L < MC_L$.

c. The completed table follows.

Quantity of Labor	Hourly Wage Rate	Total Cost of Labor	Marginal Cost of Labor
0	$ 0	$ 0	
			$ 4.00
10	4	40	
			7.00
15	5	75	
			7.50
25	6	150	
			8.25
45	7	315	
			9.80
70	8	560	
			10.40
120	9	1,080	
			11.20
220	10	2,200	

    d.   The profit-maximizing quantity of sunglasses is 400 pairs, the corresponding price is $12, and the quantity of labor is 45.

Problem Relating Input Use to Production Function

4. a. With K fixed at 20, the equation for output is

$$Q_X = 20 + 100L - 0.2L^2, \text{ and}$$

$$dQ_X/dL = MP_L = 100 - 0.4L.$$

Multiplying by NMR = MR - 5 = 10, we obtain

$$MRP_L = 1,000 - 4L.$$

b.   Profit will be maximized where $MRP_L = P_L = 40$.

$1,000 - 4L = 40$, and $L = 960/4 = \underline{240}$.

c.   Where $L = 240$, output is

$$Q_x = 20 + 100(240) - 0.2(240)_2$$

$$= 20 + 24,000 - 11,520 = 12,500.$$

Therefore, $TR = \$15(12,500) = \$187,500$.

$TC = TFC + TVC = \$100,000 + 5(12,500) + 240(40) = \$172,100$.

Total profit $= (TR - TC) = \$187,500 - 172,100$

$$= \underline{\$15,400}.$$

MULTIPLE CHOICE QUESTIONS

1. **(c)**;   2. **(b)**;   3. **(a)**;   4. **(b)**;   5. **(d)**.

CHAPTER 13:   Solutions for Practice Problems

Basic Problems on Present Value and Net Present Value

1.   PV of $50,000 now = $\underline{\$50,000}$.

PV of $7,500 per year for 10 years
$= \$7,500 \times PVF_a(6\%,10)$
$= \$7,500 \times (7.3601)$
$= \underline{\$55,200.75}$.

The annuity has the larger present value.

2. $\underline{DC-10}$

$NPV = \$750,000 \times PVF_a(12\%,8) - 3,000,000$

$= \$750,000 \times 4.9676 - 3,000,000$

$= 3,725,700 - 3,000,000$

$= \underline{\$725,700}$.

Boeing 727

NPV = $560,000 X PVF_a(12%,8) - 2,200,000

 = $2,781,856 - 2,200,000

 = $581,856.

The DC-10 has the higher net present value.

3.

a. Machine A

NPV_A = $5,000 X PVF_a(10%,10) + 2,000 X PVF(10%,10)

 - 30,000

 = 5,000 X 6.1446 + 2,000 X .3855 - 30,000

 = 31,494 - 30,000

 = $1,494.

Machine B

NPV_B = $6,500 X PVF_a(10%,10) + 3,000 X PVF(10%,10)

 - 40,000

 = 6,500 X 6.1446 + 3,000 X .3855 - 40,000

 = 39,939.90 + 1,156.50 - 40,000

 = 41,096.40 - 40,000

 = $1,096.40.

b. Machine A. It has the higher NPV.

Net Present Value Problems With a Capital Budget Constraint

4.

a. NPV_X = $47,500 X PVF_a(14%,3) - 100,000

 = 47,500 X 2.3216 - 100,000

 = 110,276 - 100,000

 = $10,276.

 NPV_Y = $165,000 X PVF(14%,3) - 100,000

 = 165,000 X .6750 - 100,000

$$= 111,375 - 100,000$$

$$= \$11,375.$$

b. $\underline{IRR_X}$:

$47,500 \times PVF_a(X\%,3) = \$100,000$

$$PVF_a(X\%,3) = \frac{100,000}{47,500} = 2.1053$$

From Table in Appendix B in the text, X% is slightly over 20%.

$\underline{IRR_Y}$:

$165,000 \times PVF(X\%,3) = \$100,000$

$$PVF(X\%,3) = \frac{100,000}{165,000} = .6061$$

From Table in Appendix B in the text, X% is slightly over 18%.

c. There is a conflict between the IRR and NPV rankings in this case due to the marginal cost of capital value used and the timing of the cash flows. NPV_Y is greater than NPV_X, while IRR_X is greater than IRR_Y. In this case, the firm should choose Project Y since its NPV is higher and, therefore, it will maximize the wealth of the firm. Note, however, that it is very important that the firm estimate its MCC accurately. At a discount rate of 18%, NPV_X is greater than NPV_Y: $3,279 > $419.)

5.

a. $\underline{Project\ A}$:

$NPV_A = \$80,000 \times PVF_a(15\%,12) - 400,000$

$$= 80,000 \times 5.4206 - 400,000$$

$$= 433,648 - 400,000$$

$$= \$33,648.$$

Project B:

NPV_B = \$60,000 X PVF_a(15%,12) - 300,000

     = 60,000 X 5.4206 - 300,000

     = 325,236 - 300,000

     = \$25,236.

Project C:

NPV_C = \$50,000 X PVF_a(15%,12) - 200,000

     = 50,000 X 5.2406 - 200,000

     = 271,030 - 200,000

     = \$71,030.

Project D:

NPV_D = \$40,000 X PVF_a(15%,12) - 200,000

     = 40,000 X 5.4206 - 200,000

     = 216,824 - 200,000

     = \$16,824.

Project E:

NPV_E = \$25,000 X PVF_a(15%,12) - 100,000

     = 25,000 X 5.4206 - 100,000

     = 135,515 - 100,000

     = \$35,515.

b. The project groupings that meet the \$500,000 capital budget constraint and their associated total NPVs are as follows:

Group	Total NPV
Projects A, E	\$ 69,163
Projects B, C	\$ 96,266
Projects B, D	\$ 42,060
Projects C, D, E	\$123,369

The group with the highest total NPV is that with projects C, D, and E.

Problem Involving Calculating the Marginal Cost of Capital

6. a.

$$MCC = .30(.12)(.65) + .70(.18)$$

$$= .30(.078) + .126$$

$$= .0234 + .126$$

$$= .1494 \text{ or approximately } 15\%.$$

b.

$$NPV = \$125,000 \times PVF_a(15\%, 9) + 10,000 \times PVF(15\%, 9)$$
$$- 600,000$$

$$= 125,000 \times 4.7716 + 10,000 \times .2843 - 600,000$$

$$= 596,450 + 2,843 - 600,000$$

$$= 599,293 - 600,000$$

$$= \$-707.$$

Since NPV is less than zero, the project is not acceptable.

MULTIPLE CHOICE QUESTIONS

1. **(b)**; 2. **(c)**; 3. **(b)**; 4. **(d)**; 5. **(b)**.

CHAPTER 14: Solutions for Practice Problems

1. Basic Problem on Expected Cash Flow and Standard Deviation

  a.   <u>Project A</u>

$$X_i P_i$$

$$\$ 80,000 \times .25 = \$20,000$$
$$100,000 \times .50 = 50,000$$
$$120,000 \times .25 = \underline{30,000}$$
$$\overline{X}_A = \$100,000$$

Project B

$X_i P_i$

$	0 X .25 = $	0
	100,000 X .50 =	50,000
	200,000 X .25 =	50,000

$$\overline{X}_B = \$100,000$$

b.   Project A

P_i	$[X_i - X]$	$[X_i - X]^2$	$P_i [X_i - X]^2$
.25	-20,000	400,000,000	100,000,000
.50	0	0	0
.25	20,000	400,000,000	100,000,000

$$\sigma_A^2 = 200,000,000$$

$$\sigma_A = \$14,142.14$$

Project B

P_i	$[X_i - X]$	$[X_i - X]^2$	$P_i [X_i - X]^2$
.25	-100,000	10,000,000,000	2,500,000,000
.50	0	0	0
.25	100,000	10,000,000,000	2,500,000,000

$$\sigma_B^2 = 5,000,000,000$$

$$\sigma_B = \$70,710.68$$

c.

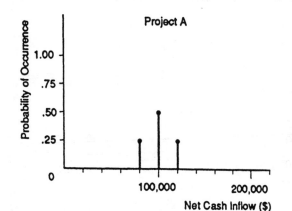

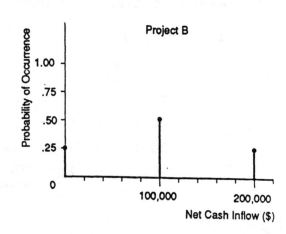

d.   Project A.   The expected net cash flow for A is greater
     than for B, their initial outlays are equal, and the risk
     is smaller with A.

2.   **Problem Using Risk-Return Indifference Curves**

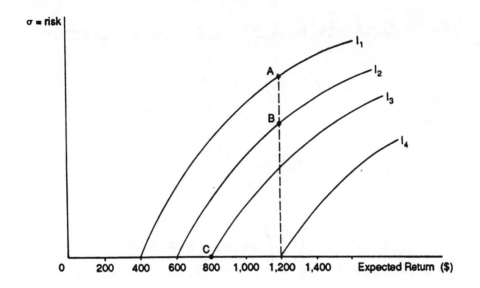

Investor will prefer C to either A or B, but B to A, since
satisfaction is higher on I_3 than on I_2 and higher on I_2 than
on I_1.

3.   **Problem Calculating NPV Using Risk-Adjusted Discount Rate**

    Jeans

NPVJ = $75,000 X PVF_a(18%,4) + 20,000 X PVF(18%,4) - 150,000

     = 75,000 X 2.6901 + 20,000 X .5158 - 150,000

     = 201,757.50 + 10,316 - 150,000

     = 212,073.50 - 150,000

     = $62,073.50

    Land

NPV_L = $480,000 X PVF(24%,4) - 150,000

     = 480,000 X .4230 - 150,000

     = $53,040

They will pick the jeans, since it has the higher NPV using
risk-adjusted discount rates.

4. Problem With Certainty Equivalent Adjustment Factors

   a.

Year	Certainty Equivalent Adjustment Factor
1	.9375
2	.9000
3	.8500
4	.8000
5	.7500

   b.

$$PV = \$75,000 \times PVF(8\%,1) + 90,000 \times PVF(8\%,2)$$
$$+ 102,000 \times PVF(8\%,3) + 96,000 \times PVF(8\%,4)$$
$$+ 90,000 \times PVF(8\%,5)$$
$$= 75,000 \times .9259 + 90,000 \times .8573 + 102,000 \times .7938$$
$$+ 96,000 \times .7350 + 90,000 \times .6806$$
$$= 69,442.50 + 77,157 + 80,967.60 + 70,560 + 61,254$$
$$= \$359,381.10$$

   c.

$$PV = \$80,000 \times PVF(15\%,1) + 100,000 \times PVF(15\%,2)$$
$$+ 120,000 \times PVF(15\%,3) + 120,000 \times PVF(15\%,4)$$
$$+ 120,000 \times PVF(15\%,5)$$
$$= 80,000 \times .8696 + 100,000 \times .7561 + 120,000 \times .6575$$
$$+ 120,000 \times .5718 + 120,000 \times .4972$$
$$= 69,568 + 75,610 + 78,900 + 68,616 + 59,664$$
$$= \$352,358$$

d. The certainty equivalent method does not automatically
    assume later cash flows are more risky than earlier cash
    flows.

e.
$$\phi_t = \frac{(1 + r)^t}{(1 + k)^t} ,$$

where r is the risk-free rate and k is a risk-adjusted
discount rate. For example,

$$\phi_1 = \frac{(1.08)}{(1.15)} = .9391, \text{ and}$$

$$\phi_2 = \frac{(1.08)^2}{(1.15)^2} = \frac{(1.1664)}{(1.3225)} = .8820.$$

MULTIPLE CHOICE QUESTIONS

   1. (d);   2. (b);   3. (c);   4. (c);   5. (a).

CHAPTER 15: Solutions for Practice Problems

1. Basic Problem Using Cost-Benefit Analysis

   a. PV of net benefits = $280,000 X PVF_a(9%,25)
                          = 280,000 x 9.8226
                          = $2,750,328

This figure is greater than the initial cost outlay so the
lake is an acceptable project.

$$\left[\frac{B}{C} = \frac{\$2,750,328}{\$2,000,000} = 1.375 > 1.\right]$$

b. PV of net benefits = $\$280,000$ X $PVF_a(14\%,25)$

$$= \$280,000 \text{ X } 6.8729$$

$$= \underline{\$1,924,412}$$

This figure is less than the initial cost outlay so the lake is no longer an acceptable project.

$$\left[\frac{B}{C} = \frac{\$1,924,412}{\$2,000,000} = 0.962 < 1.\right]$$

Cost-Benefit Problems Involving Several Projects

2.

Project A

PV of Annual Differential Benefits (B):

$\quad$ [$\$900,000$ X $PVF_a(10\%,10)$ = 900,000 X 6.1446] = $\$5,530,140$

PV of Annual Differential Costs:

$\quad$ [$\$300,000$ X $PVF_a(10\%,10)$ = 300,000 X 6.1446] = $\$1,843,380$

Initial Capital Outlay $\qquad\qquad\qquad\qquad$ = $\underline{2,000,000}$

Total Differential Costs (C) $\qquad\qquad\qquad$ = $\$3,843,380$

Net Benefit = B - C $\qquad\qquad\qquad\qquad\qquad$ = $\underline{\$1,686,760}$

$$\frac{B}{C} = \frac{\$5,530,140}{\$3,843,380} = 1.44 \quad \text{Acceptable}$$

Project B

PV of Annual Differential Benefits (B):

[$\$1,250,000$ X $PVF_a(10\%,20)$ = 1,000,000 X 8.5136] = $\$10,642,000$

PV of Annual Differential Costs:

$[\$200,000 \times PVF_a(10\%, 20) = 200,000 \times 8.5136]$ = $ 1,702,720

Initial Capital Outlay   = 8,000,000

Total Differential Costs (C)   = $ 9,702,720

Net Benefit = B - C   = $ 939,280

$\dfrac{B}{C} = \dfrac{\$10,642,000}{\$9,702,720} = 1.10$ Acceptable

Project C

PV of Annual Differential Benefits (B):

$[\$680,000 \times PVF_a(10\%, 15) = 680,000 \times 7.6061]$ = $5,172,148

PV of Annual Differential Costs

$[\$250,000 \times PVF_a(10\%, 15) = 250,000 \times 7.6061]$ = $1,901,525

Initial Capital Outlay   = 3,000,000

Total Differential Costs (C)   = $4,901,525
Net Benefit = B - C   = $ 270,623

$\dfrac{B}{C} = \dfrac{\$5,172,148}{\$4,901,525} = 1.06$ Acceptable

Project D

PV of Annual Differential Benefits (B):

$[\$700,000 \times PVF_a(10\%, 15) = 700,000 \times 7.6061]$ = $5,324,270

PV of Annual Differential Costs

$[\$300,000 \times PVF_a(10\%, 15) = 300,000 \times 7.6061]$ = 2,281,830

Initial Capital Outlay   = 3,500,000

Total Differential Costs (C)   = $5,781,830
Net Benefit = B - C   = $ -457,560

$$\frac{B}{C} = \frac{\$5,324,270}{\$5,781,830} = 0.92 \quad \text{Not Acceptable}$$

Project E

PV of Annual Differential Benefits (B):

[$625,000 X PVF$_a$(10%,20) = 625,000 X 8.5136] = $5,321,000

PV of Annual Differential Costs

[$150,000 X PVF$_a$(10%,20) = 150,000 X 8.5136] = $1,277,040

Initial Capital Outlay   =   4,000,000

Total Differential Costs (C)   = $5,277,040

Net Benefit = B - C   = $ 43,960

$$\frac{B}{C} = \frac{\$5,321,000}{\$5,277,040} = 1.01 \quad \text{Acceptable}$$

Project F

PV of Annual Differential Benefits (B):

[$330,000 X PVF$_a$(10%,2) = 330,000 X 1.7355] = $572,715

PV of Annual Differential Costs

[$50,000 X PVF$_a$(10%,2) = $50,000 X 1.7355]   = $ 86,775

Initial Capital Outlay   = $500,000

Total Differential Costs (C)   = $586,775

Net Benefit = B - C   = $-14,060

$$\frac{B}{C} = \frac{\$572,715}{\$586,775} = 0.98 \quad \text{Not Acceptable}$$

Project G

PV of Annual Differential Benefits (B):

[$1,400,000 X PVF_a(10%,20) = $1,400,000 X 8.5136] = $11,919,040

PV of Annual Differential Costs

[$500,000 X PVF_a(10%,20) = 500,000 X 8.5136]   = $ 4,256,800

Initial Capital Outlay   = $ 6,000,000

Total Differential Costs (C)   = $10,256,800

Net Benefit = B - C   = $ 1,662,240

$$\frac{B}{C} = \frac{\$11,919,040}{\$10,256,800} = 1.16 \quad \text{Acceptable}$$

Project H

PV of Annual Differential Benefits (B):

[$400,000 X PVF_a(10%,10) = 400,000 X 6.1446] = $2,457,840

PV of Annual Differential Costs

[$200,000 X PVF_a(10%,10) = 200,000 X 6.1446] = $1,228,920

Initial Capital Outlay   = $1,000,000

Total Differential Costs (C)   = $2,228,920

Net Benefit = B - C   = $ 228,920

$$\frac{B}{C} = \frac{\$2,457,840}{2,228,920} = 1.10 \quad \text{Acceptable}$$

3.

Project A

PV of Annual Differential Benefits (B):

[$900,000 X PVF_a(15%,10) = 900,000 X 5.0188] = $4,516,920

PV of Annual Differential Costs

[$300,000 X PVF_a(15%,10) = 300,000 X 5.0188] = $1,505,640

Initial Capital Outlay   = 2,000,000

Total Differential Costs (C)   = $3,505,640

Net Benefit = B - C   = $1,011,280

$$\frac{B}{C} = \frac{\$4,516,920}{\$3,505,640} = 1.29 \quad \text{Acceptable}$$

Project B

PV of Annual Differential Benefits (B):

[$1,250,000 X PVF_a(15%,20) = $1,250,000 X 6.2593] = $7,824,125

PV of Annual Differential Costs

[$200,000 X PVF_a(15%,20) = $200,000 X 6.2593]   = $ 1,251,860

Initial Capital Outlay   = $ 8,000,000

Total Differential Costs   = $ 9,251,860

Net Benefit = B - C   = $-1,427,735

$$\frac{B}{C} = \frac{\$7,824,125}{\$9,251,860} = 0.85 \quad \text{Not Acceptable}$$

Project C

PV of Annual Differential Benefits (B):

[$680,000 X PVF_a(15%,15) = 680,000 X 5.8474] = $3,976,232

PV of Annual Differential Costs

[$250,000 X PVF_a(15%,15) = 250,000 X 5.8474] = $1,461,850

Initial Capital Outlay   = <u>3,000,000</u>

Total Differential Costs (C)   = $4,461,850

Net Benefit = B - C   = $ -485,618

$$\frac{B}{C} = \frac{\$3,976,232}{\$4,461,850} = 0.89 \quad \text{Not Acceptable}$$

Project D

PV of Annual Differential Benefits (B):

[$700,000 X PVF_a(15%,15) = 700,000 X 5.8474] = $4,093,180

PV of Annual Differential Costs

[$300,000 X PVF_a(15%,15) = 300,000 X 5.8474] = $ 1,754,220

Initial Capital Outlay   = <u>$ 3,500,000</u>

Total Differential Costs (C)   = $ 5,254,220

Net Benefit = B - C   = $-1,161,040

$$\frac{B}{C} = \frac{\$4,093,180}{\$5,254,220} = 0.78 \quad \text{Not Acceptable}$$

Project E

PV of Annual Differential Benefits (B):

[$625,000 X PVF_a(15%,20) = 625,000 X 6.2593] = $ 3,912,062.50

PV of Annual Differential Costs

[$150,000 X PVF_a(15%,20) = 150,000 X 6.2593] = $ 938,895.00

Initial Capital Outlay   = <u>$ 4,000,000.00</u>

Total Differential Costs (C)   = $ 4,938,895.00

Net Benefit = B - C   = $-1,026,832.50

$$\frac{B}{C} = \frac{\$3,912,062.50}{\$4,938,895.00} = 0.79$$

Project F
PV of Annual Differential Benefits (B):

[$330,000 X PVF_a(15%,2) = 330,000 X 1.6257] = $536,481

PV of Annual Differential Costs

[$50,000 X PVF_a(15%,2) = 50,000 X 1.6257]   = $ 81,285

Initial Capital Outlay   = $500,000

Total Differential Costs (C)   = $581,285

Net Benefit = B - C   = $-44,804

$$\frac{B}{C} = \frac{\$536,481}{\$581,285} = 0.92 \quad \text{Not Acceptable}$$

Project G
PV of Annual Differential Benefits (B):

[$1,400,000 X PVF_a(15%,20) = 1,400,000 X 6.2593] = $8,763,020

PV of Annual Differential Costs

[$500,000 X PVF_a(15%,20) = 500,000 X 6.2593] = $3,129,650

Initial Capital Outlay   = 6,000,000

Total Differential Costs (C)   = $9,129,650

Net Benefit = B - C   = $ -366,360

$$\frac{B}{C} = \frac{\$8,763,020}{\$9,129,650} = 0.96 \quad \text{Not Acceptable}$$

Project H

PV of Annual Differential Benefits (B):

$[\$400,000 \times PVF_a(15\%,10) = 400,000 \times 5.0188] = \$2,007,520$

PV of Annual Differential Costs

$[\$200,000 \times PVF_a(15\%,10) = 200,000 \times 5.0188] = \$1,003,760$

Initial Capital Outlay   = $\underline{1,000,000}$

Total Differential Costs (C)   = $2,003,760

Net Benefit = B - C   = $\underline{\underline{\$\quad 3,760}}$

$$\frac{B}{C} = \frac{\$2,007,520}{\$2,003,760} = 1.002 \quad \text{Acceptable}$$

Only projects **A** and **H** are acceptable.

4.

The following groups are combinations of acceptable projects that meet the budget constraint.

Group I: Projects A and G

Total Net Benefit = $1,686,760 + 1,662,240 = $3,349,000

$$\frac{B}{C} = \frac{\$17,449,180}{\$14,100,180} = 1.24$$

Group II: Project B

Total Net Benefit = $939,280

$$\frac{B}{C} = \frac{\$10,642,000}{\$9,702,720} = 1.10$$

Group III: Projects C, E, and H

Total Net Benefit = $270,623 + 43,960 + 228,920 = $543,503

$$\frac{B}{C} = \frac{\$5,172,148 + 5,321,000 + 2,457,840}{\$4,901,525 + 5,277,040 + 2,228,920} = \frac{\$12,950,988}{\$12,407,485} = 1.04$$

Group I with projects A and G has the highest total net benefit and the highest B/C ratio.

The combinations of projects listed below require a total initial outlay that is less than $8,000,000. They also have a lower total net benefit than does Group I with projects A and G.

Group IV: Projects A, C, and H   (Total Outlay = $6,000,000)

Total Net Benefit = $1,686,760 + 270,623 + 228,920 = $2,186,303

$$\frac{B}{C} = \frac{\$5,530,140 + 5,172,148 + 2,457,840}{\$3,843,380 + 4,901,525 + 2,228,920} = \frac{\$13,160,128}{\$10,973,825} = 1.20$$

Group V: Projects A, E, and H   (Total Outlay = $7,000,000)

Total Net Benefit = $1,686,760 + 43,960 + 228,920 = $1,959,640

$$\frac{B}{C} = \frac{\$5,530,140 + 5,321,000 + 2,457,840}{\$3,843,380 + 5,277,040 + 2,228,920} = \frac{\$13,308,980}{\$11,349,340} = 1.17$$

Group VI: Projects G and H   (Total Outlay = $7,000,000)

Total Net Benefit = $1,662,240 + 228,920 = $ 1,891,160

$$\frac{B}{C} = \frac{\$11,919,040 + 2,457,840}{\$10,256,800 + 2,228,920} = \frac{\$14,376,880}{\$12,485,720} = 1.15$$

5.

Enlarge Convention Center

PV of Annual Differential Benefits (B):

[$500,000 X PVF_a(12%,10) = 500,000 X 5.6502] = $2,825,100

PV of Annual Differential Costs

[$60,000 X PVF_a(12%,10) = 60,000 X 5.6502]   = $ 339,012

Initial Capital Outlay   =   2,000,000
Total Differential Costs (C)   = $2,339,012
Net Benefit = B - C   = $ 486,088

$$\frac{B}{C} = \frac{\$2,825,100}{\$2,339,012} = 1.21$$

Build a New Park

PV of Annual Differential Benefits (B):

[$450,000 X PVF_a(12%,10) = $450,000 X 5.6502] = $2,542,590

PV of Annual Differential Costs

[$40,000 X PVF_a(12%,10) = 40,000 X 5.6502]   = $ 226,008

Initial Capital Outlay   =   1,950,000
Total Differential Costs (C)   = $2,176,008

Net Benefit = B - C   = $ 336,582

$$\frac{B}{C} = \frac{\$2,542,590}{\$2,176,008} = 1.17$$

New Fire Station

PV of Annual Differential Benefits (B):

[$600,000 X PVF_a(12%,10) = 600,000 X 5.6502] = $3,390,120

PV of Annual Differential Cost

[$70,000 X PVF_a(12%,10) = 70,000 X 5.6502]   = $ 395,514

Initial Capital Outlay   =   1,900,000

Total Differential Costs (C)   = $2,295,514

Net Benefit = B - C   = $1,094,606

$$\frac{B}{C} = \frac{\$3,390,120}{\$2,295,514} = 1.48$$

Drainage Project

PV of Annual Differential Benefits (B):

[$500,000 X PVF_a(12%,10) = 500,000 X 5.6502] = $2,825,100

PV of Annual Differential Costs

[$50,000 X PVF_a(12%,10) = 50,000 X 5.6502] = $ 282,510

Initial Capital Outlay   =   2,050,000

Total Incremental Costs (C)   = $2,332,510

Net Benefit = B - C   = $ 492,590

$$\frac{B}{C} = \frac{\$2,825,100}{\$2,332,510} = 1.21$$

Build Elevated Railway

PV of Annual Differential Benefits (B):

[$650,000 X PVF_a(12%,10) = 650,000 X 5.6502] = $3,672,630

PV of Annual Differential Costs
[$100,000 X PVF_a(12%,10) = 100,000 X 5.6502] = $ 565,020

Initial Capital Outlay   =   2,100,000

Total Differential Costs (C)   = $2,665,020

Net Benefit = B - C   = $1,007,610

$$\frac{B}{C} = \frac{\$3,672,630}{\$2,665,020} = 1.38$$

The new fire station has the highest total net benefit and the highest B/C ratio and therefore should be chosen.

MULTIPLE CHOICE QUESTIONS

1. (c);   2. (d);   3. (b);   4. (d);   5. (c).

CHAPTER 16:

MULTIPLE CHOICE QUESTIONS

1. (b);   2. (c);   3. (d);   4. (a);   5. (b).